SLOW COOKER
RECIPE BOOK

100 Slow Cooker Recipes

ABOUT LIANA'S KITCHEN

Liana's Kitchen is a food blog filled with simple and easy to make recipes. Traditional favourites that everyone can make at home with minimal fuss and expense.

If you've not visited, come and check us out at LianasKitchen.co.uk

If you have any questions about any of these recipes, or about slow cooking in general, please feel free to contact me at liana@lianaskitchen.co.uk

BONUS GIFTS

For a free blank recipe template and meal planner, please head over to;

LianasKitchen.co.uk/slow-cooker-bonus

CONTENTS

CHAPTER 1

USING YOUR SLOW COOKER

THE RECIPES

Follow these recipes as a guide for what you can make in your own slow cooker.

Each cooker will vary slightly and you should always refer to the manufacturer's manual when deciding how long to cook something for, and at what temperature.

The majority of these recipes are made to serve 4 - but you can reduce or increase the quantities accordingly. We used a 6L slow cooker, but any size slow cooker can be used.

The good news is you can be quite flexible with your cooking times - use the ones in the recipes as a guideline. It's also worth noting that slow cooker models can vary in how quickly they cook - as you use your slow cooker more you will get to know how long you need to cook certain foods. If in doubt with meat, use a meat thermometer.

ADAPTING A RECIPE

If your favourite recipe isn't in this book, you will be pleased to know that many recipes can be adapted for the slow cooker. The best kinds are casseroles and stews, soups, curries - recipes that don't require too much intervention.

However, I was quite surprised when I first got our slow cooker to discover just how much I could make in it. After a lot of reading and experimentation, I have made breads, cakes, jam, fudge and some lovely hot drinks. The slow cooker is quite a versatile kitchen appliance.

Another point to note is that when adapting a recipe you need to reduce any liquid by at least a third, sometimes more.

As a general rule, use the following conversions;

ORIGINAL	LOW	HIGH
15 TO 30 MINS	4 TO 6 HOURS	1 TO 2 HOURS
30 MINS TO 1 HOUR	5 TO 7 HOURS	2 TO 3 HOURS
1 TO 2 HOURS	6 TO 8 HOURS	3 TO 4 HOURS
2 TO 4 HOURS	8 TO 10 HOURS	4 TO 6 HOURS

THE SLOW COOKER LID

Try not to remove the lid whilst it is cooking - unless the recipe calls for it.

Each time you remove the lid, heat will escape, adding a further 20 minutes to your cooking time.

Some recipes do advise to remove the lid before the end to allow the sauce to thicken up.

There are exceptions, for example, the fudge recipe requires you to leave the lid off for the whole time – but the general rule is leave it on and don't be tempted to lift it up for a sneaky peek – unless you need to add something in.

ADDING INGREDIENTS

Some ingredients don't do well if they are put in the slow cooker at the beginning of the cooking time.

Foods like onions, potatoes, carrots (and other root veg), can be put in from the beginning, but more delicate vegetables like peas and corn would do better if added during the last 20 to 30 minutes of cooking time.

Dairy can be added to a slow cooker, but only in recipes that are cooked on the low setting and for a shorter cooking.

Fresh herbs can be added and stirred in just before serving.

TO BROWN OR NOT TO BROWN

This is a personal preference and there are no strict rules.

Personally, I like slow cooker recipes that are quick to prepare and so I often skip the browning step!

All of the recipes in this book can be made without any pre browning required.

Having said that, there are certain meats and vegetables that might taste better, depending on your opinion of course, when they have been browned.

Searing meat in a separate pan before putting it in the slow cooker can produce extra flavour, but it doesn't have to be done.

Browning the meat beforehand will change the texture of the meat and of course the colour. Sausages definitely taste better if they are browned before adding them in, or they come out very pale and the texture is soft. Likewise, I like to brown off meatballs before adding them to the slow cooker as they have a tendency to fall apart otherwise.

Onions and garlic can be cooked on the stove beforehand too, this will improve the flavour of the final dish, but again, it is not compulsory.

HOW TO THICKEN UP SAUCES

If by the end of the cooking time the sauce is a little thin for your liking you can thicken it up with a little corn flour or potato starch.

Just mix a teaspoon with a little cold water until it forms a paste. Then stir it into the slow cooker and allow it to cook for a little longer. Add more corn flour if required.

You can also add some gravy granules to thicken it up. Alternatively, roll the meat in a little flour before adding it.

If you have a slow cooker with a built in 'sear' function you can also use this to reduce the sauce. Or, you can transfer to a pan to simmer down (although this is my last resort, remember, less washing up and all that!)

WHAT MEAT SHOULD I USE?

The great thing about slows cookers is you can use cheaper cuts of meat and it still tastes great!

Chicken thighs, beef brisket, pork shoulder, lamb shoulder, neck and shanks are all great to use.

You can use chicken breasts too, just reduce the cooking time to avoid them drying out.

Use my meat quantities as an estimation - I believe they are enough to feed 4, but you can adjust according to you - also, adding in extra beans or pulses help bulk out a meal.

CAN I COOK WHOLE JOINTS?

Yes, you can. You can cook any joint of meat this way.

You can just put them in as they are, or add seasoning and herbs.

Some joints, such as a whole roast chicken, might benefit from a little time under a grill at the end to crisp it up – but it's not compulsory.

The meat comes out so tender, it quite literally falls off the bone. A meat thermometer is useful for checking that a whole joint is cooked through.

ROOT VEGETABLES

It can take a while to cook root vegetables in a slow cooker. Cut them to equal sizes so they are ready at the same time as well as add them at the beginning of the cook time.

DRIED PULSES

Beans and pulses are perfect for slow cooking.

Check the packet instructions for each one, but as a general rule, dried beans and peas tend to require soaking overnight in cold water.

Make sure there is enough water to cover them in the slow cooker, with the liquid coming above the beans.

Beans will generally take about 6 to 8 hours on low in a slow cooker.

RICE AND PASTA

Make sure you thoroughly rinse rice before putting it in. Only cook pasta and rice for a short time on a high setting, or add it towards the end of the cook time.

HOW FULL CAN THE SLOW COOKER BE?

For your slow cooker to work at its maximum efficiency you should try to at least half fill it. You can fill the slow cooker up to the top, but if you have a lot of liquid in there, for example, when you are making soups and some stews, leave at least a 5cm gap at the top to allow for it bubbling up.

PREPARING AHEAD OF TIME

If mornings are a rush, prepare everything the night before. Then all you have to do is throw it all in and switch it on!

REHEATING SLOW COOKER MEALS

A slow cooker should not be used to reheat a meal. Reheat any cooked food in a pot on the stove, bringing it to the boil before reducing the heat and leaving it to simmer for about 10 to 15 minutes. Make sure it is thoroughly cooked through and only reheat it once.

CHAPTER 2

SOUP RECIPES

MAKING SOUP IN A SLOW COOKER

Almost any soup can be made in a slow cooker, with soups containing root vegetables and meats that require longer slow cooking times working the best.

Although a slow cooker soup is similar to a conventional pot on the stove recipe, the process does differ.

Follow these tips and you'll soon be cooking all your favourite soups in a slow cooker!

SLOW COOKER SOUP – STEP BY STEP

1. Prepare the ingredients - try to chop them to similar sizes.

2. Add any root vegetables first, followed by meat (if using), herbs and spices, aromatics, stock. Save dairy until the end.

3. Switch the slow cooker on – low is preferred for a more flavoursome soup, but high is fine to use if you are short on time.

4. For smooth soups, blend (a hand blender is easier to use).

5. Thicken soup if required - cornflour or potato starch both work well.

6. Serve soup with optional garnishes – croutons, a swirl of cream, fresh herbs, nuts and seeds.

LEEK & POTATO SOUP

SERVINGS: 4 - 6

PREP TIME: 20 MINUTES

COOK TIME: 6 TO 8 HOURS ON LOW

INGREDIENTS

- 8 potatoes, chopped
- 3 leeks, chopped
- 1 onion, chopped
- 2 tbsp. butter
- 2 x vegetable stock pots/cubes
- 1 litre boiling water
- Seasoning - salt/celery salt/black pepper

METHOD

1. Peel and chop potatoes to equal sizes and add to slow cooker.

2. Add leeks, onions and butter.

3. Dilute 2 stock cubes in 1 litre of boiling water.

4. Add stock to the slow cooker so that it just covers the ingredients. Add any preferred seasoning and stir everything together.

5. Set off on high for 4 hours, or low for 6 - 8 hours.

6. When finished - the ingredients should be soft - blend with a stick blender, or, transfer to a large blender. If you prefer a chunkier consistency, you might choose just to pulse or mash the soup with a potato masher.

Notes

As a variation, stir in some diced Stilton cheese at the end and garnish with some chopped crispy bacon.

MINESTRONE SOUP

SERVINGS: 4 - 6

PREP TIME: 20 MINUTES

COOK TIME: 6 TO 8
HOURS ON LOW

INGREDIENTS

- 1 tbsp. olive oil
- 2 onions, chopped
- 2 cloves garlic, crushed
- 3 rashers smoky bacon, chopped (optional)
- 2 small courgettes, chopped
- 3 celery sticks, chopped 3 carrots, chopped
- 2 x 400g tomatoes/passata
- ½ tsp dried oregano 2 bay leaves
- 1 litre of chicken or vegetable stock (from 2 stock pots/cubes)
- 100g dried soup pasta*
- Large handful of spinach
- Salt and pepper to season

METHOD

1. Peel and chop potatoes to equal sizes and add to slow cooker.

2. Add leeks, onions and butter.

3. Dilute 2 stock cubes in 1 litre of boiling water.

4. Add stock to the slow cooker so that it just covers the ingredients. Add any preferred seasoning and stir everything together.

5. Set off on high for 4 hours, or low for 6 - 8 hours.

6. When finished - the ingredients should be soft - blend with a stick blender, or, transfer to a large blender. If you prefer a chunkier consistency, you might choose just to pulse or mash the soup with a potato masher.

Notes

You can use any pasta for minestrone soup, if you can't get small soup pasta then use macaroni, or broken up spaghetti.

POTATO & BACON SOUP

SERVINGS: 4

PREP TIME: 20 MINUTES

COOK TIME: 6 HOURS ON LOW

INGREDIENTS

- 6 slices bacon, chopped
- 1 onion, finely diced
- 6 large potatoes, peeled and cubed
- 2 celery stalks, chopped
- 1 tsp garlic powder
- 1 tsp dried mixed herbs
- 700ml chicken or vegetable stock seasoning
- 400ml double or single cream
- 50g plain flour
- 1 tsp chopped fresh chives (optional)

METHOD

1. Fry the bacon and onion in a frying pan. Drain away excess fat.

2. Transfer to the slow cooker and add remaining ingredients, apart from the cream and flour.

3. Set off on low for 6 hours.

4. 20 minutes before the end, whisk the flour and cream together.

5. Add to the slow cooker and stir together.

6. Replace lid and cook for a further 20 minutes.

7. Serve with sprinkled fresh chives (optional)

Notes

As a variation, stir in some diced Stilton cheese at the end and garnish with some chopped crispy bacon.

BEEF & BARLEY SOUP

SERVINGS: 4

PREP TIME: 10 MINUTES

COOK TIME: 7 TO 8 HOURS ON LOW

INGREDIENTS

- 1 kg beef, diced
- 1 onion, chopped
- 2 cloves garlic, crushed
- 3 carrots, chopped
- 3 celery stick, chopped
- 2 large potatoes, diced
- 120g pearl barley
- 2 tsp Worcestershire sauce
- 1.5L beef stock
- 1 tsp dried thyme
- Salt and pepper to taste

METHOD

1. Pearl barley shouldn't require soaking, just a good rinse under the tap.

2. Add all the ingredients to the slow cooker and stir.

3. Set off on low for 7 to 8 hours. If the sauce is too thin stir in some beef gravy granules or some corn flour (1 tbsp. corn flour mixed with 2 tbsp. water).

4. Serve as it is or with some warm crusty bread to dip in!

Notes

Substitute the beef with lamb cubes for a change of soup.

SPICED LENTIL & CARROT SOUP

SERVINGS: 4

PREP TIME: 10 MINUTES

COOK TIME: 6 TO 8
HOURS ON LOW

INGREDIENTS

- 800g carrots, washed and chopped, or coarsely grated
- 200g split red lentils, washed
- 700ml hot vegetable stock
- 1 tbsp. ground cumin
- 1 tsp chilli flakes
- Salt and pepper to taste

METHOD

1. Add everything to the slow cooker and set off on high for 3 hours or low for 6 to 8 hours, until the lentils are soft and tender.

2. Mash or blend when finished to the consistency you prefer.

3. Optionally stir in some yoghurt, milk or coconut milk. Season according to taste. Add additional chilli flakes if required.

Notes
You can use 1 to 2 tbsp. curry powder instead of the cumin, or leave the spices out completely!

BUTTERNUT SQUASH SOUP

SERVINGS: 4

PREP TIME: 20 MINUTES

COOK TIME: 6
HOURS ON LOW

INGREDIENTS

- 1 large butternut squash (approx. 1kg), peeled & chopped
- 1 onion, sliced
- 3 cloves garlic, crushed
- 200g carrots, chopped
- 1.2L vegetable stock
- Salt and pepper to season

METHOD

1. Add all the ingredients to the slow cooker. The stock should just about cover the butternut squash.

2. Set off on low for 6 to 8 hours or high for 4 hours.

3. Blend with a hand blender directly in the slow cooker, or wait until it has cooled enough to put in a blender.

4. Season with salt and pepper if required.

Notes

Turn it into a curried butternut squash soup by adding in 1 to 2 tbsp. curry powder.

CHICKEN AND CHICKPEA SOUP

SERVINGS: 4

PREP TIME: 10 MINUTES

COOK TIME: 6 HOURS ON LOW

INGREDIENTS

- 2 chicken breasts
- 1 onion, sliced
- 2 cloves garlic, crushed
- 2 celery sticks, sliced
- 400g chopped tomatoes
- 400g can chickpeas
- 150g red lentils, rinsed
- 1 tsp ground cumin
- 1 tsp ground ginger
- ½ tsp ground cinnamon
- ½ tsp ground coriander
- 1L chicken stock

METHOD

1. Add everything to the slow cooker and mix it together.

2. Set off on low for 6 hours, or high for 4 hours.

3. When the chicken is soft and cooked through, shred it with some forks - you can either do this directly in the slow cooker or remove it to a separate bowl/plate if easier.

4. Mix the shredded chicken with the soup and season if required.

CHICKEN NOODLE SOUP

SERVINGS: 4

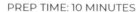

PREP TIME: 10 MINUTES

COOK TIME: 6
HOURS ON LOW

INGREDIENTS

- 6-8 boneless chicken thighs
- 1 onion, chopped
- 4 cloves garlic, crushed
- 2 large carrots, chopped
- 2 bay leaves
- 1 tsp dried mixed herbs
- 1L chicken stock
- Salt & pepper to taste
- 150g egg noodles
- Fresh herbs to serve (optional)

METHOD

1. Add everything to the slow cooker apart from the noodles.

2. Set off on low for 6 hours, or high for 3 to 4 hours.

3. Lift the lid 15 to 20 minutes before the end of the cooking time and shred the chicken with 2 forks. Add the noodles and cook for the remaining time, or until the noodles are soft.

VEGETABLE SOUP

SERVINGS: 4

PREP TIME: 15 MINUTES

COOK TIME: 6
HOURS ON LOW

INGREDIENTS

- 1 onions, chopped
- 2 cloves garlic, crushed
- 3 bay leaves
- 6 carrots, sliced
- 3 sticks celery, sliced
- 2 large potatoes, diced
- 150g runner beans
- 400g tinned tomatoes
- 1 tbsp. tomato puree
- 1L vegetable stock
- 1 tsp dried mixed herbs
- Salt and pepper according to taste.

METHOD

1. Add all the ingredients to the slow cooker and stir together.

2. Set off on low for 6 hours, or high for 3 hours.

3. Serve the soup chunky, or, using a hand blender, whizz it smooth before serving. Add more seasoning if required.

Notes

You can substitute any of these vegetables with your favourites, or what is in season. Some vegetables such as broccoli are best added in the last 20 to 30 minutes to prevent them from going too soft.

If the soup is too thick add some more stock and stir through. If it is too thin, thicken it up with some corn flour, or cook with lid off for final 30 minutes.

PEA AND HAM

SERVINGS: 4

PREP TIME: 10 MINUTES

COOK TIME: 8 TO 10
HOURS ON LOW

INGREDIENTS

- 200g bacon lardons or 5 rashers, sliced
- 300g split green peas, rinsed
- 1 onion, sliced
- 3 celery sticks, sliced
- 2 bay leaves
- 1 tsp dried thyme
- 1.5L chicken or vegetable stock
- Salt and pepper to taste

METHOD

1. Cook the bacon in a pan until crispy.

2. Add all the ingredients to the slow cooker, including the bacon.

3. Cook on low for 8 to 10 hours, or high for 4 - 6 hours.

4. Remove bay leaves and either mash with a potato masher, or use a stick blender to partially blend. Taste and season some more if required.

5. Serve with crusty bread.

CHAPTER 3

CHICKEN RECIPES

SWEET & SOUR CHICKEN

SERVINGS: 4

PREP TIME: 10 MINUTES

COOK TIME: 5-6
HOURS ON LOW

INGREDIENTS

- 8 small boneless chicken thighs/4 chicken breasts
- 1 clove garlic, crushed
- 1 onion, chopped
- 2 carrots, chopped
- 1 red pepper, deseeded and sliced
- 1 green pepper, deseeded and sliced

For the sweet and sour sauce:

- 3 tbsp. ketchup
- 1 can (250ml) pineapple pieces
- 2 tbsp. corn flour
- 150ml apple cider vinegar
- 100g brown sugar
- 1 tbsp. soy sauce

METHOD

1. Prepare the sweet and sour sauce by mixing all the ingredients together. If you prefer a less tangy taste to your sweet and sour, reduce the amount of cider vinegar to 100ml.

2. Add the chicken to the slow cooker. Add the garlic, onions and carrots. You can optionally add the peppers now or add them 30 minutes before the end of the cooking time, depending on how soft you like them.

3. Pour the sweet and sour sauce over the top and place the lid on.

4. Set off on low for 5 to 6 hours, or high for 4 hours.

5. Serving Suggestions: noodles or rice.

Notes

In a rush? Don't have all the ingredients? Grab a jar of premade sweet and sour sauce and add that instead of making your own.

THAI RED CURRY

SERVINGS: 4

PREP TIME: 10 MINUTES

COOK TIME: 6-8
HOURS ON LOW

INGREDIENTS

- 400ml coconut milk
- 4-6 tbsp. Thai red curry paste*
- 1 red chilli, sliced (optional)
- 4 cloves garlic, crushed
- 2 kaffir lime leaves (or juice of 1 lime)
- 1 tbsp. fresh root ginger, grated/1tsp ground ginger
- 1 tbsp. fish sauce
- 150ml chicken stock
- 100g mange tout or sugar snap peas**
- 4 chicken breast/8 small boneless chicken thighs
- Basil leaves for garnish

METHOD

1. In the slow cooker, mix together the coconut milk, Thai red curry paste, chilli, garlic, lime leaves (or juice of 1 lime), ginger, fish sauce and chicken stock.

2. Add the chicken.

3. Set off on low for 6-8 hours or on high for 4 hours.

4. Half an hour before the end lift the lid and stir in the mange tout or sugar snap peas. If the sauce is too runny at this stage stir in a corn flour slurry (1 tbsp. corn flour mixed with 1 tbsp. water).

5. Serve with rice and/or naan bread.

Notes

*Thai red curry paste - how much you put in will be dependent on how spicy you like your curries.

**Vegetables - you can substitute for your favourites, or what you have to hand. Sweet peppers are a great alternative or addition.

CHICKEN CHASSEUR

SERVINGS: 4

PREP TIME: 10 MINUTES

COOK TIME: 6 - 8 HOURS ON LOW

INGREDIENTS

- 400g chopped tomatoes
- 200ml hot chicken stock
- 150ml dry white wine (optional)
- 1 tbsp. tomato purée
- 1 onion, chopped
- 2 garlic cloves, crushed
- 200g baby chestnut/button mushrooms, halved
- 4 carrots, sliced
- ½ tsp dried thyme, or 2 fresh thyme sprigs
- 1 bay leaf
- 4-8 boneless chicken thighs or breast

METHOD

1. Add chopped tomatoes, hot stock, dry white wine (if using) and tomato puree to slow cooker and stir together.

2. Add in the onion, garlic, carrots, mushrooms and herbs and stir.

3. Place chicken in the slow cooker and gently mix it in so it is covered in the sauce.

4. Cook on low for 6-8 hours or high for 3 hours (thighs). 4 hours on low, 2-3 hours high for (breast).

5. Serving Suggestions: mashed potato or rice.

HONEY & MUSTARD

SERVINGS: 4

PREP TIME: 10 MINUTES

COOK TIME: 6-8
HOURS ON LOW

INGREDIENTS

- 8 boneless chicken thighs/4 large chicken breasts
- 2-4 tbsp. honey
- 2 tbsp. Dijon mustard
- 4 spring onions, sliced
- 2 cloves garlic, crushed
- 150ml chicken stock
- Optional: green peas, broccoli

METHOD

1. Optionally sear the chicken before adding it to the slow cooker.

2. In a jug make up the stock with hot water. Add in the honey, mustard, garlic and spring onions. Add in any salt and pepper according to taste.

3. Pour the stock mixture over the chicken in the slow cooker.

4. Cook on low for 6-8 hours or high for 3 hours (thighs). 4 hours on low, 2-3 hours high for (breast).

5. In the last 30 minutes, lift the lid off to allow the sauce to thicken up. If you are adding peas or broccoli you can add them now. If the sauce is too runny for you make up a little corn flour slurry according to the packet instructions, or alternatively stir in a little cream.

6. Serving suggestions: rice, noodles or mashed potatoes.

CHICKEN & CHORIZO

SERVINGS: 4

PREP TIME: 15 MINUTES

COOK TIME: 6-8 HOURS LOW

INGREDIENTS

- 150g chorizo, cut into 1cm slices
- 1 chicken stockpot or cube
- 2 red onions, sliced
- 2 red/yellow peppers, deseeded, chopped
- 2 cloves garlic, crushed
- 2 x 400g tin of chopped tomatoes
- 2 tsp smoked paprika
- 8 boneless chicken thighs
- Fresh flat-leaf parsley - optional garnish

METHOD

1. Dry fry the chorizo slices in a pan for a few minutes to release the oils.

2. Dissolve the stockpot/cube in 50ml of boiling water.

3. Add the onions, peppers, garlic, tomatoes, stock and paprika into the slow cooker and stir to combine.

4. Add the chicken and chorizo.

5. Add lid and set the slow cooker off for 6 hours on low. If the sauce is too thin use 1 tbsp. of corn flour combined with 1 tbsp. water and mix in the sauce. If you don't have any corn flour, you can leave the lid off the slow cooker for a further 30 minutes.

THAI GREEN CURRY

SERVINGS: 4

PREP TIME: 20 MINUTES

COOK TIME: 4 TO 5 HOURS LOW

INGREDIENTS

- 8 chicken thighs
- 1 stick lemongrass
- 4 tbsp. Thai green curry paste*
- 400ml coconut milk (1 tin)
- 2 green chillies, sliced (deseed for a milder taste)
- 1 tbsp. fish sauce
- 2 kaffir lime leaves
- 1 green pepper, deseeded and sliced 100g baby corn
- 100g mange tout

METHOD

1. Place the chicken in the slow cooker.

2. Remove the outer leaf, and slice the lemongrass stalk, discarding the bottom centimetre.

3. Add the Thai green curry paste, coconut milk, green chillies, fish sauce and lime leaves to the slow cooker. Optionally add the peppers, baby corn and mange tout in now, or, for a firmer texture, add them 30 minutes before the end of the cooking time.

4. Cook on low for 4 to 5 hours, or high for 3 to 4 hours.

Notes

Not all Thai green curry paste is created equal! If you find this recipe doesn't come out as spicy or flavoursome as you would like you might need to experiment with some different brands or have a go at making your own! Also, if using homemade curry paste you may want to use more, as the flavours are not quite as intense as shop bought paste.

CAJUN CHICKEN CASSEROLE

SERVINGS: 4

PREP TIME: 5 MINUTES

COOK TIME: LOW 8 HOURS
OR HIGH 4 HOURS

INGREDIENTS

- 400g chopped tomatoes
- 1 - 2 tbsp. Cajun seasoning*
- 1 onion, chopped
- 1 sweet pepper, chopped
- 8 chicken thighs
- Salt and pepper to season

METHOD

1. In the slow cooker, mix together the chopped tomatoes, Cajun seasoning, onion and sweet pepper.

2. Add the chicken and set off on low for 6-8 hours or high for 4 hours.

3. Serve with rice or potato wedges.

Notes

If you don't have any Cajun seasoning use: 1 tsp paprika, 1 tsp cayenne pepper, 1/2 tsp cumin, 1/2 tsp oregano, 1/2 tsp garlic powder

LEMON & GARLIC CHICKEN

SERVINGS: 4

PREP TIME: 20 MINUTES

COOK TIME: LOW
4-6 HOURS

INGREDIENTS

- 8 boneless chicken thighs
- 2 tsp dried mixed herbs
- 4 tbsp. fresh lemon juice
- 2 tbsp. of honey
- 4 cloves garlic, crushed
- 1 chicken stock pot/cube in 50ml boiling water
- Salt and pepper according to taste
- 1 tbsp. fresh parsley, chopped (optional)

METHOD

1. Season the chicken with the mixed herbs and add to the slow cooker.

2. Dissolve the chicken stock in 50ml of boiling water and add lemon juice, honey and garlic and pour over the chicken.

3. Set off on low for 4-6 hours, or high for 3 hours.

4. About 20 minutes before the end, add the fresh parsley. If the sauce seems too runny at this stage you can leave the lid off for the remaining time, and/or stir in some corn flour (1 tbsp. corn flour + 1 tbsp. water mixed together).

HUNTERS CHICKEN

SERVINGS: 4

PREP TIME: 10 MINUTES COOK

COOK TIME: 4 HOURS ON LOW

INGREDIENTS

- 4 chicken breasts
- 4-8 rashers of bacon 200ml BBQ sauce*

METHOD

1. Wrap 1 or 2 bacon rashers around each chicken breast. If you have any, use a cocktail stick to secure each rasher of bacon in place.

2. Place the chicken breasts and bacon in the slow cooker.

3. Pour the BBQ sauce over the chicken breasts.

4. Cook on low for 4 hours, or high for 2-3 hours.

5. Serve with potato wedges, mashed potatoes or chips.

Notes

Optionally sprinkle some Granny Smith apples, peeled and grated across the top.

*Either use shop bought BBQ sauce or make your own.

SALSA GARLIC CHICKEN

SERVINGS: 4

PREP TIME: 5 MINUTES

COOK TIME: LOW
4 TO 6 HOURS

INGREDIENTS

- 8 boneless chicken thighs
- 300g salsa (shop-bought or homemade)
- 6 cloves garlic, crushed
- 1 tsp paprika
- 2 red onions, sliced

METHOD

1. Add chicken thighs to the slow cooker.

2. Add salsa, garlic, paprika and sliced red onion.

3. Stir everything together and set off on low for 4 to 6 hours, or high for 3 to 4 hours.

4. Serve with rice, potato wedges or in a tortilla wrap - you can shred the chicken before putting it in.

Notes
Add a chopped red or green chilli for some extra heat!

CHILLI PEANUT COCONUT CHICKEN

SERVINGS: 4

PREP TIME: MINUTES

COOK TIME: LOW
4 TO 6 HOURS

INGREDIENTS

- 400ml coconut milk
- 4 tbsp. peanut butter
- 4 cloves garlic, crushed
- 1 tbsp. brown sugar
- 2 tbsp. soy sauce
- 2 tbsp. lime juice
- 1 tbsp. chilli powder
- 1 tsp dried chilli flakes
- 8 boneless thighs
- 1 red chilli, sliced

METHOD

1. In a bowl, stir together coconut milk, peanut butter, garlic, brown sugar, soy sauce, lime juice, chilli powder and dried chilli flakes. Make sure it is well mixed together.

2. Lay the chicken on the base of the slow cooker and pour the sauce over the top and add the sliced red chilli.

3. Cook on low for 4 to 6 hours. Remove the lid from the slow cooker and using 2 forks, shred the chicken and stir into sauce. If the sauce needs thickening up leave the lid off or stir in some corn flour to thicken

4. Serve with rice or noodles and optionally garnish with some fresh coriander.

Notes

For a milder taste deseed the chilli, or leave it out of the recipe.

CHICKEN IN GREEN PESTO

SERVINGS: 4

PREP TIME: 5 MINUTES

COOK TIME: LOW
4 TO 6 HOURS

INGREDIENTS

- 4 chicken breasts
- 8 tbsp. green pesto
- 2 cloves of garlic, crushed
- 100g mozzarella

METHOD

1. Place the chicken thighs/breasts in the slow cooker.

2. Spoon the pesto over the chicken, evenly distributing as much as you can.

3. Sprinkle the crushed garlic over the top.

4. Cook on low for 4 to 6 hours.

5. 10 to 15 minutes before you are ready to switch the slow cooker off, remove the lid and sprinkle the mozzarella across the chicken and allow it to melt. Replace the lid and cook until the cheese has melted.

6. Serve with rice, pasta or mashed potatoes.

WHOLE ROAST CHICKEN

SERVINGS: NA

PREP TIME: 10 MINUTES

COOK TIME: LOW
8 HOURS

INGREDIENTS

- 1 whole raw chicken (size to fit slow cooker)
- 1 onion, chopped
- 1 tbsp. dried mixed herbs (or seasoning of your choice)

METHOD

1. Season the whole chicken according to your tastes. Either use some dried mixed herbs, or you can just use salt and pepper, or whatever your favourite herbs and spices are!

2. Place the whole chicken in the slow cooker. You can optionally place the chicken joint on some rolled up foil balls, or on top of chopped vegetables such as onions and carrots.

3. Cook on low for 8 hours or high for 4-5 hours. Check the chicken is cooked through by piercing it with a sharp knife and seeing if the juices run clear. Alternatively, use a meat thermometer.

4. If you want to crisp up the chicken skin, brush with a little oil and place under a grill for 3 to 5 minutes.

Notes

When you cook a whole chicken in a slow cooker it can sometimes fall apart when you remove it.

One way around this is to use a sling. You can either buy a purpose made silicone sling or make your own from rolled up foil.

CHINESE CHICKEN CURRY

SERVINGS: 4

PREP TIME: 10 MINUTES

COOK TIME: LOW
6 HOURS

INGREDIENTS

- 8 boneless chicken thighs
- 2 cloves garlic, crushed
- 1 tbsp. fresh root ginger, grated/1tsp ground ginger
- 85g Chinese curry powder*
- 1 chicken stock cube/pot 350ml boiling water
- 1 tbsp. soy sauce
- 2 sweet peppers (any colours), thinly sliced
- 150g frozen peas
- Salt & pepper to season

METHOD

1. Mix the Chinese curry powder with the water, chicken stock pot, soy sauce, garlic and ginger.

2. Place chicken thighs in the slow cooker and pour liquid mixture over the top.

3. Set off on low for 4-6 hours or high for 3 hours.

4. Half an hour before the end, add the sliced peppers and frozen peas. If the sauce is too thin at the end of the cooking time, leave the lid off for the last 30 minutes and put the slow cooker on high.

5. Alternatively, stir in a corn flour slurry to thicken up.

6. Serve with rice, noodles or over a baked potato.

Notes

Chinese curry powder/concentrate: the most popular and easy to get brands are Mayflower and Goldfish. I get mine from Iceland but they are also available online.

BBQ CHICKEN LEGS

SERVINGS: 4

PREP TIME: 5 MINUTES

COOK TIME: 5 TO 6
HOURS ON LOW

INGREDIENTS

- 1kg chicken drumsticks
- 2 tsp mild chilli powder
- 300ml BBQ sauce

METHOD

1. Rub the mild chilli powder over the drumsticks and add to the slow cooker.

2. Pour the BBQ sauce over the chicken legs, covering them all.

3. Cook for 5 to 6 hours on low, or 3 to 4 hours on high.

4. Optional: at the end of the cooking time transfer the chicken legs to a baking tray and coat with a little more BBQ sauce. Grill for 5 minutes or until the skin crisps up.

5. Serve with potato wedges, mashed potato, rice or chips.

Notes
You can use either shop-bought BBQ sauce, or you can make your own.

CHICKEN FAJITAS

SERVINGS: 4

PREP TIME: 10 MINUTES

COOK TIME: LOW
FOR 4 HOURS

INGREDIENTS

- 4 chicken breasts
- 3-4 tbsp. fajita spice mix
- 1 onion, chopped
- 1 red pepper, sliced
- 1 green pepper, sliced 1 yellow pepper, sliced
- 400g tinned tomatoes

METHOD

1. Lay chicken breasts in the slow cooker.

2. Sprinkle with the fajita mix.

3. Add the chopped onions, peppers and tomatoes - stir everything together.

4. Place the lid on the slow cooker and set off on low for 4 hours, or high for 2-3 hours.

5. If the sauce is too runny, leave the lid off the slow cooker and cook on high for about 20 to 30 minutes to thicken it up.

6. Serve with tortilla wraps, salsa, lettuce and grated cheese, or load on top of jacket potatoes.

Notes

You may need to ladle out some of the sauce if serving with tortillas.

There might be too much liquid, making the wraps soggy!

CHICKEN TIKKA MASALA

SERVINGS: 4

PREP TIME: 20 MINUTES

COOK TIME: LOW
6 HOURS

INGREDIENTS

- 8 boneless chicken thighs/4 chicken breasts
- 1 medium onion, chopped
- 4 cloves garlic, crushed
- 1 tbsp. fresh ginger, grated (or 1 tsp ground ginger)
- 4 tbsp. tikka masala spice mix (see notes to make your own)
- 400g tin tomatoes or passata
- 150ml cream/yoghurt/coconut milk
- Fresh coriander for garnish (optional)

METHOD

1. Add all the ingredients to the slow cooker apart from the yoghurt and coriander.

2. Stir the ingredients to combine.

3. Set off on low for 6 hours, or high for 4 hours.

4. If required at the end of the cooking time, leave the lid off for 20 minutes to thicken up the sauce.

5. Stir in yoghurt/cream/coconut milk and fresh coriander if using.

Notes

Tikka spice mix: 2 tsp garam masala, 3 tsp ground coriander, 3 tsp ground cumin, 2 tsp chilli powder, 1 tsp garlic powder, 1 tsp ground turmeric, 1 tsp ground ginger, pinch of salt

TUNISIAN CHICKEN STEW

SERVINGS: 4

PREP TIME: 10 MINUTES

**COOK TIME: LOW
4 TO 6 HOURS**

INGREDIENTS

- 400g chopped tomatoes/passata
- 1 tsp turmeric
- 1 tsp ground cinnamon
- ½ tsp salt
- 4 tbsp. harissa paste
- 2 onions, sliced
- 2 cloves garlic, crushed
- 8 boneless chicken thighs

METHOD

1. Stir the tomatoes/passata, spices, salt and harissa paste together in the slow cooker.

2. Add the onions and garlic.

3. Add the chicken thighs and cover them in the sauce.

4. Set off on low for 6 to 8 hours or high for 4 hours.

Notes
Serve with couscous and mint yoghurt
(mix 3 tbsp. fresh chopped mint leaves in
with 8 tbsp. plain yoghurt)

CHICKEN CASSEROLE

SERVINGS: 4

PREP TIME: 20 MINUTES

COOK TIME: LOW FOR 8 HOURS

INGREDIENTS

- 8 boneless chicken thighs/4 breasts
- 4 carrots, chopped
- 2 stalks celery, sliced
- 2 cloves garlic, crushed
- 1 or 2 onions, peeled and sliced
- 500g new potatoes, cut in half
- 1 tbsp. mustard
- 2 tsp dried mixed herbs
- 2 bay leaves
- 2 chicken stock cubes/pots
- 300ml boiling water
- Gravy granules to thicken

METHOD

1. Add all the ingredients to the slow cooker, apart from the gravy granules.

2. Give everything a gentle stir to mix together.

3. Place the lid on the slow cooker and set off on low for 8 to 10 hours, or high for 4 to 6 hours.

4. 30 minutes before the end, take the lid off and stir in 2 to 3 tbsp. of gravy granules.

5. Leave the lid off for the last 30 minutes to allow the stock to thicken up. If you aren't able to wait 30 minutes, just stir in the gravy granules until the desired consistency is reached.

6. Remove the bay leaves.

Notes

You can add any vegetables you have available for this chicken casserole. If you don't add any potatoes to the slow cooker you can serve it with some mashed potato or crusty bread.

CHAPTER 4

TURKEY RECIPES

TURKEY CROWN

SERVINGS: 6-8

PREP TIME: 5 MINUTES

COOK TIME: 5 HOURS

INGREDIENTS

- 2kg turkey crown (approx.)
- 2 onions
- 1 tbsp. olive oil
- 2 tsp dried mixed herbs
- Seasoning

METHOD

1. Brush with olive oil and season with herbs, salt, pepper, or your choice of herbs/spices.

2. Chop onions and place in the bottom of the slow cooker. Place the turkey crown on top of onions.

3. Put the lid on the slow cooker and cook on high for 5 hours. Baste the turkey with the juices in the slow cooker once or twice during the cooking time.

4. After 5 hours, check the turkey is cooked all the way through. Use a meat thermometer if you can, it should be at least 70°C. If you don't have a thermometer check the turkey has no pink bits and the juices run clear. If undercooked, return to the slow cooker for an extra half an hour.

5. Leave the turkey to rest at room temperature for at least 30 minutes before serving.

TURKEY STUFFED PEPPERS

SERVINGS: 4-6

PREP TIME: 15 MINUTES

COOK TIME: 4-5 HOURS

INGREDIENTS

- 4-6 sweet bell peppers (any colours)
- 500g turkey mince
- 1 onion, finely sliced
- 2 cloves garlic, crushed
- 2 tsp dried mixed herbs
- 2 tbsp. tomato puree
- 1 tbsp. Worcestershire sauce
- 100g cooked rice
- 100g cheddar, grated
- 400ml chicken stock or passata

METHOD

1. Slice the tops off the peppers and remove the seeds and stem from the inside, taking care not to split the pepper.

2. In a bowl, mix together the turkey, onion, garlic, herbs, tomato puree, Worcestershire sauce, cooked rice and half of the grated cheese.

3. Scoop the mixture into the peppers. Pour the chicken stock or passata in the base of the slow cooker.

4. Place the peppers in the slow cooker in an upright position. Place the lid on top and set off on low for 4 to 5 hours, or high for 3 hours.

5. Sprinkle remaining grated cheese on top of peppers and replace the lid for a further xx minutes, or until the cheese melts.

TURKEY CHILLI

SERVINGS: 4

PREP TIME: 20 MINUTES

COOK TIME: 6 TO 8
HOURS ON LOW

INGREDIENTS

- 500g turkey thigh mince 1 onion, chopped
- 2 cloves garlic, crushed
- 3 tbsp. chilli powder
- 1 tsp ground cumin
- 1 tsp cayenne pepper
- 1 x 400g tinned tomatoes
- 1 x can kidney beans*
- 100ml chicken stock (from 1 stock cube/pot)
- Seasoning according to taste

METHOD

1. Add all the ingredients to the slow cooker and stir to combine.

2. Set off on low for 6 to 8 hours, or high for 4 hours.

3. Serve with rice or over a jacket potato.

Notes
You can use any beans that you have - borlotti or black beans can be a good substitute.

MEXICAN TURKEY & BACON WRAPS

SERVINGS: 4

PREP TIME: 10 MINUTES

COOK TIME: 6 TO 8
HOURS ON LOW

INGREDIENTS

- 500g turkey mince
- 200g smoked bacon lardons (or bacon rashers, chopped)
- 150ml barbecue sauce
- 3-4 tbsp. taco seasoning*
- 1 sweet pepper (any colour), deseeded and sliced

METHOD

1. Optionally fry the bacon lardons first (they will taste better if crispy!)

2. Add everything to the slow cooker and stir together.

3. Cook on low for 6 to 8 hours or high for 4 hours.

4. Serve in warm tortilla wraps with sour cream, cheese, guacamole, or over a jacket potato.

Notes

You can either substitute the taco seasoning for fajita seasoning, or, make your own:

1 tbsp. chilli powder, 1tsp cumin, 1tsp paprika, ½ tsp chilli flakes, 1 tsp garlic powder, ½ tsp onion powder, ½ tsp oregano, ½ tsp salt, ½ tsp black pepper.

CHAPTER 5

BEEF RECIPES

Moroccan Beef & Sweet Potato Stew

Beef Tacos

Meatballs in Tomato Sauce

Thai Red Curry Meatballs

Chilli Con Carne

Spaghetti Bolognese

Beef Curry

Beef Rendang

Beef & Ale Stew

Chipotle Mexican Beef Stew

Curried Beef and Chickpea

Jamaican Beef & Bean

Beef Bourguignon

Lasagne

Classic Beef Stew

Roast Beef

MOROCCAN BEEF AND SWEET POTATO STEW

SERVINGS: 4

PREP TIME: 20 MINUTES

COOK TIME: 6 TO 8
HOURS ON LOW

INGREDIENTS

- 750g beef, diced
- 1 medium onion, chopped
- 4 cloves garlic, crushed
- 2 sweet potatoes, peeled and cubed
- 2 carrots, sliced
- 1 tbsp. tomato puree
- 1 x 400g chopped tomatoes
- 2 tsp ground cumin
- 1 tsp ground cinnamon
- 1 tsp paprika
- 75g raisins

METHOD

1. Add everything to the slow cooker and stir together.

2. Set off on low for 6 - 8 hours, or high for 4 hours.

BEEF TACOS

SERVINGS: 4

PREP TIME: 10 MINUTES

COOK TIME: 6 TO 8 HOURS ON LOW

INGREDIENTS

- 500g minced beef 1 onion, sliced
- 2 cloves garlic, crushed
- 1 green pepper, sliced
- 1 red pepper, sliced
- 1 tbsp. tomato puree
- 3 to 4 tbsp. taco seasoning*
- 100ml beef stock (from 1 stock cube)

METHOD

1. Add everything to the slow cooker, apart from the peppers and stir together.

2. Set off on low for 6 to 8 hours, or high for 4 hours. Add the peppers in the last 20 to 30 minutes.

3. If the sauce is too runny, reduce it by leaving the lid off for the last 30 minutes or transfer to a pan and simmer on low heat.

4. Serve in crunchy taco shells with salsa, guacamole, lettuce and cheese melted over the top!

Notes

Taco Seasoning - you can buy this premade in most supermarkets, or you can make your own with; 1 tbsp. chilli powder, 1 tsp cumin, 1 tsp paprika, ½ tsp chilli flakes, 1 tsp garlic powder, ½ tsp onion powder, ½ tsp oregano½ tsp salt, ½ tsp black pepper.

MEATBALLS IN TOMATO SAUCE

SERVINGS: 4

PREP TIME: 10 MINUTES

COOK TIME: 4 TO 5
HOURS ON LOW

INGREDIENTS

- 24 meatballs (approx. either pre-prepared or homemade)
- 1 tbsp. dried Italian herbs
- 2 x 400g tomato passata tinned tomatoes 1tbsp tomato puree
- 1 onion
- 1 clove garlic
- Basil leaves (optional, for garnish)

METHOD

1. Gently sear the meatballs before adding them to the slow cooker - this is optional but I prefer to seal the meat to reduce the risk of the meatballs falling apart in the slow cooker.

2. Add the sauce ingredients straight to the slow cooker and mix them together.

3. Transfer the meatballs to the slow cooker so that they are submerged in the sauce and set off on low for 4 to 5 hours.

5. Remove the lid and gently stir the sauce around - take care not to break up the meatballs.

Notes

Serve over cooked spaghetti and sprinkle with grated cheese and fresh basil leaves. For minimal preparation, you can substitute with a jar of tomato pasta sauce.

THAI RED CURRY MEATBALLS

SERVINGS: 4

PREP TIME: 10 MINUTES

COOK TIME: 4 TO 5
HOURS ON LOW

INGREDIENTS

- 12 - 24 meatballs (either pre-prepared or homemade)
- 2 cloves garlic, crushed
- 4 tbsp. Thai red curry paste
- 400ml coconut milk
- 1 tbsp. fresh root ginger, grated/1 tsp ground ginger
- 1 small red chilli, deseeded and finely chopped
- Juice from half a lime
- 1 tbsp. fish sauce
- Fresh coriander - optional garnish

METHOD

1. I always brown off the meatballs in a pan to seal them. This prevents them from potentially breaking up when in the slow cooker.

2. Add all the ingredients, apart from the meatballs to the slow cooker and mix together.

3. Add the meatballs to the sauce and cook on low for 4 to 5 hours, or high for 2 to 3 hours.

4. Serving Suggestion: Garnish with freshly chopped basil or coriander and serve with rice.

Notes

To make your own Thai meatballs: use 500g of fresh beef/pork mince and mix with 50g dried breadcrumbs, 1tbsp Thai red curry paste, 1 tbsp. fish sauce, ½ tsp ground ginger, 1 clove garlic, crushed and a pinch of salt. Mix together all the ingredients and form the mixture into about 10-12 round balls using your hands. Double up to make 24 meatballs.

CHILLI CON CARNE

SERVINGS: 4

PREP TIME: 10 MINUTES

COOK TIME: 6 TO 8 HOURS ON LOW

INGREDIENTS

- 500g-750g minced beef
- 2 onions, chopped
- 2 cloves garlic, crushed
- 1 red pepper, sliced
- 2-3 tbsp. mild chilli powder
- 1 tsp smoked paprika
- 1 tsp ground cumin
- 1 tbsp. Worcestershire sauce
- 1 beef stock cube/pot
- 400g tin red kidney beans
- 400g tin chopped tomatoes
- 2 tbsp. tomato puree
- Salt and pepper to season

METHOD

1. Add all the ingredients to the slow cooker pot and stir to combine.

2. Set off on low for 6 to 8 hours, or high for 3 hours.

3. If the sauce is too thin after the cooking time leave the lid off for a further 20 - 30 minutes, or stir in 1 to 2 tbsp. of beef gravy granules.

4. Serve with your choice of side - tortilla chips, rice, baked potato etc.

SPAGHETTI BOLOGNESE

SERVINGS: 4

PREP TIME: 10 MINUTES

COOK TIME: 7 TO 10 HOURS ON LOW

INGREDIENTS

- 1 tbsp. olive oil
- 500g-750g lean beef steak mince
- 400g tin chopped tomatoes
- 400g passata
- 3 tbsp. tomato puree
- 1 onion, chopped
- 1 red pepper, deseeded and chopped
- 3 bay leaves
- 3 cloves garlic, crushed
- 1 tsp mixed dry herbs
- 1 beef stock cube or pot

METHOD

1. Add all the ingredients, including the mince and onions, to your slow cooker and stir together.

2. Set on low for 7 to 10 hours or high for 5 hours.

3. Serve with cooked spaghetti, grated cheese and garlic bread/dough balls!

BEEF CURRY

SERVINGS: 4

PREP TIME: 10 MINUTES

COOK TIME: 8 TO 10
HOURS ON LOW

INGREDIENTS

- 750g diced beef
- 1 x 400g chopped tomatoes
- 1 onion, chopped
- 4 tbsp. curry powder
- 2 cloves garlic, grated
- 1 tbsp. fresh ginger, grated
- 1 fresh red chilli, sliced (deseed if you prefer a milder taste)

METHOD

1. Add all the remaining ingredients to the slow cooker and give everything a good stir.

2. Put the lid on and set off on low for 8 to 10 hours, or high for 4 hours. Optionally stir in some yoghurt before serving

BEEF RENDANG

SERVINGS: 4

PREP TIME: 10 MINUTES

COOK TIME: 6 TO 8
HOURS ON LOW

INGREDIENTS

- 750g diced beef
- 1 onion, chopped
- 1 jar of rendang paste* (approx. 180g - 200g)
- 1 x 400g tin coconut milk
- 1 tbsp. lime juice
- 1 tsp salt
- 1 tbsp. light brown sugar
- 1 cinnamon stick
- 1 tbsp. ground cumin
- 2 tbsp. ground coriander
- 2 tsp turmeric

METHOD

1. To make the curry, optionally seal the beef with the spices by briefly frying with a bit of oil.

2. Mix everything in the slow cooker, submerging the beef last.

3. Cook on high for 4 hours, or on low for 6-8 hours.

4. If necessary, leave the lid off the slow cooker for the last 30 minutes to thicken the sauce. Serve with rice or noodles.

Notes

You can make your own rendang paste by adding the following to a food processor and pulsing to a paste: 3 shallots (or 1 onion), 4 cloves garlic, 1-inch ginger (or galangal if available), 4 red chillies, 1 lemongrass stalk, chopped (ends removed).

BEEF & ALE STEW

SERVINGS: 4   PREP TIME: 10 MINUTES   COOK TIME: 8 TO 10 HOURS ON LOW

INGREDIENTS

- 750g stewing beef*, diced
- 2 red onions, chopped
- 2 cloves garlic, crushed
- 1 tsp dried mixed herbs
- 150g small button mushrooms (optional)
- 150g carrots, chopped
- 3 tbsp. tomato puree
- 2 bay leaves
- 400ml brown ale

METHOD

1. Add all the ingredients to the slow cooker and stir to combine.

2. Cook on low for 8 hours or high for 4 hours. Remove the bay leaves before serving.

3. Tastes great with mashed potato or chunky slices of fresh bread.

Notes

You can use a beef joint such as brisket or silverside.

CHIPOTLE MEXICAN BEEF STEW

SERVINGS: 4

PREP TIME: 20 MINUTES

COOK TIME: 8 HOURS ON LOW

INGREDIENTS

- 2 cans chopped tomatoes
- 1-2 tbsp. chipotle paste
- Juice of 1 lime
- 1 tbsp. smoked paprika
- 1 tsp ground cumin
- 1 tsp chilli powder
- 2 tsp onion powder
- 2 tsp garlic powder
- 100ml beef stock (made from 1 stock pot)
- 500g - 700g diced beef/joint of beef
- 1 onion, sliced
- 4 cloves garlic, crushed
- Seasoning according to taste

METHOD

1. In a bowl or jug mix together the chopped tomatoes, chipotle paste, lime juice, spices and stock.

2. Add the beef joint, or diced beef to the slow cooker, together with the chopped onions, crushed garlic and any seasoning.

3. Pour the stock and tomato mixture over the top of the beef.

4. Put the lid on the slow cooker and cook on low for 8 hours, or high for 4 hours.

5. At the end of the cooking time, using 2 forks, shred it.

Notes
Serve with rice or over a jacket potato.
Use just 1tbsp of chipotle paste for a milder taste.
Optionally add in 1 or 2 sliced green chillies for some extra spice.

CURRIED BEEF AND CHICKPEA STEW

SERVINGS: 4

PREP TIME: 10 MINUTES

COOK TIME: 6 TO 8
HOURS ON LOW

INGREDIENTS

- 500g beef mince
- 1 x 400g tin chickpeas, drained
- 2 cloves garlic, crushed
- 1 onion, chopped
- 1 sweet red pepper, sliced
- 1 x 400g tinned tomatoes/passata
- 1 tbsp. tomato puree
- 2 tbsp. curry spice blend 100ml beef stock

METHOD

1. Make up the beef stock by adding 1 beef stock cube, or pot, to 100ml of boiling water.

2. Add all the remaining ingredients to the slow cooker.

3. Pour in the stock and stir to combine.

4. Set the slow cooker off on low for 6 to 8 hours.

JAMAICAN BEEF & BEAN

SERVINGS: 4

PREP TIME: 15 MINUTES

COOK TIME: 6 TO 8
HOURS ON LOW

INGREDIENTS

- 500g diced beef or minced beef
- 1 butternut squash, about 500-700g
- 1 onion, chopped
- 1 cloves garlic, crushed
- 1 tbsp. fresh root ginger, grated (or 1tsp ground ginger)
- 1 sweet pepper, deseeded and sliced
- 1 tbsp. thyme
- 2 tbsp. curry powder
- 4 tbsp. tomato puree
- 1 x 400g chopped tomatoes
- 1 x 400g chickpeas, drained
- 1 x 400g black-eyed beans, drained
- Salt and pepper to season

METHOD

1. Peel and chop the butternut squash.

2. Add everything to the slow cooker and stir together.

3. Set off on low for 6 to 8 hours, or high for 4 hours.

4. Serve with rice or potatoes.

Notes
Substitute butternut squash with pumpkin if available.

BEEF BOURGUIGNON

SERVINGS: 4

PREP TIME: 15 MINUTES

COOK TIME: 6 TO 8
HOURS ON LOW

INGREDIENTS

- 1 tbsp. oil
- 750g diced beef
- 150g bacon lardons, or rashers, chopped
- 1 tbsp. plain flour
- 200ml red wine
- 10 small shallots, peeled
- 3 cloves garlic, crushed
- 2 large carrots, sliced
- 2 tbsp. tomato puree
- 2 bay leaves
- 1 beef stock cube in 250ml boiling water
- 2 tsp dried mixed herbs
- 200g mushrooms, halved or quartered
- Salt and pepper to taste

METHOD

1. Heat up the oil in a frying pan and brown the diced beef - about 5 minutes.

2. Transfer the beef to the slow cooker, leaving the oil and juices in the pan.

3. Add the shallots and bacon to the pan and gently cook until the bacon is brown before adding in the garlic, mushrooms and flour.

4. Stir everything together and fry for a further minute.

5. Add in the carrots, wine, stock, tomato puree and herbs and any seasoning. Bring to the boil before taking off the heat.

6. Pour over the beef in the slow cooker and cook on low for 6 to 8 hours, or high for 4-6 hours.

7. If the sauce is too runny leave the lid off for the last 20 to 30 minutes, stir in some beef gravy granules to thicken it up or make up a corn flour slurry to stir in.

Notes

Serve with mashed potato and the sauce from the slow cooker as gravy!

LASAGNE

SERVINGS: 4

PREP TIME: 20 MINUTES

COOK TIME: 4
HOURS ON LOW

INGREDIENTS

- 750g beef mince
- 1 onion, chopped
- 2 garlic cloves, crushed
- 400g tomato passata
- 1 tbsp. tomato puree
- 2 tsp dried herbs
- 700g (approx.) lasagne sauce/ cheese sauce
- Lasagne pasta sheets (one packet if using fresh)
- Parmesan, grated (optional)

METHOD

1. Brown the mince in a pan with oil, and add onions and garlic, sautéing until soft and fragrant.

2. Stir in tomato puree, passata and dried herbs, and take off the heat.

3. Put the first layer, the mince, in the slow cooker. Cover with lasagne sheets - these can be fresh or dried.

4. Add a layer of cheese/lasagne/white sauce, and roughly smooth out over the pasta so all of it is covered. Optional: sprinkle grated parmesan over each layer.

5. Repeat until you run out of ingredients, but make sure the last layer is the cheese/lasagne sauce.

6. Cook on low for 4 hours, or 2 hours on high, although taste is improved significantly when cooked on low for longer.

CLASSIC BEEF STEW

SERVINGS: 4

PREP TIME: 10 MINUTES

COOK TIME: 8 TO 10
HOURS ON LOW

INGREDIENTS

- 500g-700g diced stewing beef
- 800g casserole vegetables*
- 2 bay leaves
- 2 tbsp. Worcestershire sauce
- 2 tsp dried mixed herbs
- 2 beef stock cubes/pots
- 500ml boiling water
- Gravy granules or corn flour to thicken (optional)

METHOD

1. Add all the ingredients to the slow cooker and stir round to make sure everything is mixed together.

2. Set off on low for 8 to 10 hours, or high for 4 hours.

3. To thicken up the stew, remove the lid for the last 30 minutes and switch the slow cooker to high. Add gravy granules or corn flour at this stage to thicken up even more.

Notes

*choose your vegetables according to what is available and what you prefer. Options can include; carrots, leeks, celery, potatoes, swede, onions.

ROAST BEEF

SERVINGS: 4

PREP TIME: 10 MINUTES

COOK TIME: 7 TO 8
HOURS ON LOW

INGREDIENTS

- Beef joint*
- 2 onions, chopped
- 4 cloves garlic, crushed
- 1 beef stock pot or cube in 500ml water
- 150ml red wine - optional
- Carrots, Parsnips, Celery - optional
- Seasoning/Herbs/Spices

METHOD

1. Optionally sear the beef joint in 2tbsp oil, dusted in 2tbsp plain flour + seasoned.

2. Make up the stock using 1 stockpot or cube in 500ml hot water.

3. Add everything to the slow cooker. If you are cooking any green vegetables with your beef (broccoli, green beans etc.) add them 20 minutes before the end of the cooking time.

4. Cook on low for 7 to 8 hours, or high for 5 hours.

5. Leave the beef to stand for 10 minutes before carving - cut thick slices to avoid crumbling.

6. Serve with the juices from the slow cooker by adding some gravy granules or a corn flour slurry to thicken it up.

Notes
Brisket is a good choice as is silverside.

CHAPTER 6

PORK RECIPES

BBQ Pork Ribs

Chilli Peanut Pork

Sausage Casserole

Piri Piri Pork

Pork in Maple Syrup

Sweet Chilli Onion Pork

Pork & Bramley Apple

Sunday Roast Pork Joint

BBQ Pulled Pork

Jerk Pork & Pineapple Salsa

Pulled Curried Pork

Gammon

Pork Casserole

BBQ PORK RIBS

SERVINGS: 4

PREP TIME: 10 MINUTES

COOK TIME: 7 TO 8
HOURS ON LOW

INGREDIENTS

- 700g-1.5kg pork ribs
- 300ml barbecue sauce
- 1 tbsp. Worcestershire sauce
- 3 cloves garlic, crushed
- 1 tbsp. smoked paprika

METHOD

1. In a bowl, add the BBQ sauce, Worcestershire sauce, garlic and paprika to the slow cooker and mix together.

2. Add the pork ribs to the slow cooker. Pour ¾ of the sauce (approx.) over the ribs, reserving the remainder for later.

3. Set the slow cooker off on low for 7 - 8 hours, or high for 3 to 4 hours.

4. Carefully remove the ribs from the slow cooker, taking care not to disturb them too much (or the meat will fall off!) Place them on a lined baking tray.

5. Spoon out some of the juice from the slow cooker and mix it in with the reserved sauce. Baste the cooked ribs with it. Place the baking tray under a grill for 5 to 10 minutes or until the ribs start to crisp up. Serve with potato wedges.

CHILLI PEANUT PORK

SERVINGS: 4

PREP TIME: 15 MINUTES

COOK TIME: 6 TO 8
HOURS ON LOW

INGREDIENTS

- 750g-1kg pork, diced
- 200ml chicken or pork stock
- 50ml soy sauce
- 100g smooth peanut butter
- 2 tbsp. honey
- 4 cloves garlic, crushed
- 1 tbsp. grated fresh ginger/1 tsp ground ginger
- 1 tsp dried chilli flakes
- 1 sweet red pepper, deseeded and thinly sliced

METHOD

1. Make up the stock with boiling water in a jug. Stir in the soy sauce, peanut butter, honey, garlic, ginger and chilli flakes. Stir until the peanut butter has dissolved.

2. Add the pork, stock mixture and peppers to the slow cooker and gently stir to combine.

3. Set off on low for 6-8 hours, or until the pork is soft and tender.

4. Serving suggestion - tastes great with noodles!

SAUSAGE CASSEROLE

SERVINGS: 4

PREP TIME: 20 MINUTES

COOK TIME: 7 TO 9
HOURS ON LOW

INGREDIENTS

- 12 thick pork sausages
- 1 red onion, chopped
- 1 red pepper, deseeded/chopped
- 400g tin of chopped tomatoes
- 3 medium carrots, chopped
- 2 cloves garlic, crushed
- 1 tsp dried mixed herbs
- 400ml beef stock

METHOD

1. Brown off the sausages under a grill or in a little oil in a pan. Drain off any fat and add to the slow cooker.

2. Add the remaining ingredients and stir to mix.

3. Cook on low for 7 to 9 hours, or high for 4 hours.

PIRI PIRI PORK

SERVINGS: 4

PREP TIME: 10 MINUTES

COOK TIME: 6 TO 8
HOURS ON LOW

INGREDIENTS

- 750g-1 kg diced pork
- 4 tbsp. piri piri seasoning
- 400g tin chopped tomatoes/ passata
- 2 cloves garlic, crushed
- 1 red pepper, sliced

METHOD

1. Season pork with piri piri seasoning and add to the slow cooker.

2. Add tomatoes/passata, garlic and pepper.

3. Set off on high for 4 - 6 hours or low for 6 to 8 hours. When finished, serve in brioche buns, with rice or potato wedges.

Notes

You could also use a whole pork joint and turn it into a 'pulled pork' recipe. Leave it to cook for a little longer until the pork is soft enough to pull apart.

PORK IN MAPLE SYRUP

SERVINGS: 4

PREP TIME: 10 MINUTES

COOK TIME: 6 TO 8
HOURS ON LOW

INGREDIENTS

- 1 tbsp. soy sauce
- 2 tbsp. maple syrup
- 3 tbsp. tomato ketchup
- 2 cloves garlic, crushed
- 1 red onion, sliced
- 4- 6 boneless pork chops

METHOD

1. Mix the soy sauce, maple syrup, tomato ketchup, garlic and onion in the slow cooker.

2. Add the pork to the slow cooker and coat it in the sauce.

3. Set off on low for 6 hours.

4. Serve with roasted vegetables and mashed potato.

SWEET CHILLI ONION PORK CHOPS

SERVINGS: 4

PREP TIME: 10 MINUTES

COOK TIME: 6
HOURS ON LOW

INGREDIENTS

- 2 tbsp. Worcestershire sauce
- 1 tbsp. tomato puree
- 1 tbsp. apple cider vinegar
- 2 tbsp. brown sugar
- ½ tsp salt
- ½ tsp black pepper
- 1 tsp dried chilli flakes
- 4 - 6 boneless pork chops
- 2 onions, sliced
- 2 tbsp. butter

METHOD

1. Add the Worcestershire sauce, tomato puree, apple cider vinegar, brown sugar, salt, pepper and dried chilli flakes to the slow cooker.

2. Stir together until combined. Lay the pork chops on top of the sauce mix followed by the sliced onions. Dot the butter over the top of the onions.

3. Place the lid on and set off on low for 6 hours. Tastes great with mashed potato or chips!

PORK AND BRAMLEY APPLE

SERVINGS: 4

PREP TIME: 10 MINUTES

COOK TIME: 6 TO 8
HOURS ON LOW

INGREDIENTS

- 4 x pork shoulder steaks
- 2 sticks celery, sliced
- 2 Bramley apples, chopped into wedges
- 1 tsp dried sage*
- 1 bay leaf*
- 1 tbsp. mustard
- 100ml vegetable or chicken stock (from 1 stock cube/pot)
- 4 tbsp. double cream (optional)

METHOD

1. Add pork to the slow cooker. Add remaining ingredients to the slow cooker, apart from the optional double cream (if using), covering the pork.

2. Set off on low for 6 to 8 hours, or high for 4 hours.

3. If you are adding cream, remove the pork from the sauce and stir it in before replacing the pork. Serve with mashed or roast potatoes!

Notes

*If you don't have any dried sage or bay leaves you can add 1 tsp of dried mixed herbs instead.

SUNDAY PORK ROAST JOINT

SERVINGS: 4

PREP TIME: 15 MINUTES

COOK TIME: 6 TO 8
HOURS ON LOW

INGREDIENTS

- 1kg-2kg pork joint
  - Seasoning*
- 1 onions, chopped
  - 4 carrots, sliced
  - 2 bay leaves
- 300ml pork/chicken/vegetable stock**

METHOD

1. Season the pork joint according to your tastes (check notes).

2. Place the pork in the slow cooker and place the onions and carrots around it.

3. Pour the stock in and add the bay leaves.

4. Set off on low for 8 hours.

5. For crispy crackling, place under the grill for 15 to 20 minutes at the end - either remove the skin and do it on its own, or place the whole pork joint in a baking tray. Rub the skin with salt first.

Notes

*Seasoning - this can be as simple as some salt and pepper, or you could add some of your favourite dried herbs, garlic granules, celery salt etc.

**It's possible to slow cook without the addition of any stock - but I find a little bit for this recipe helps it stay moist.

Optionally add some chopped up apples at the start.

BBQ PULLED PORK

SERVINGS: 4

PREP TIME: 10 MINUTES

COOK TIME: 8 TO 10
HOURS ON LOW

INGREDIENTS

- 1.5kg - 2kg boneless shoulder pork joint
- 2 tsp smoked paprika
- 1 clove garlic, crushed
- 2 tbsp. brown sugar
- 1 tbsp. white wine vinegar
- 1 tbsp. Worcestershire sauce
- 200ml tomato ketchup

METHOD

1. In a bowl/jug, mix the paprika, garlic, brown sugar, white wine vinegar, Worcestershire sauce and tomato ketchup.

2. Place the pork joint in the slow cooker. Pour the sauce over the top of the pork. Place the lid on the slow cooker and cook on high for 4 to 6 hours or 8 to 10 hours on low.

3. Remove the lid, and using 2 forks, shred the pork and mix it into the sauce.

4. Serve with brioche buns and coleslaw with some potato wedges on the side.

JERK PORK & PINEAPPLE SALSA

SERVINGS: 4

PREP TIME: 20 MINUTES

COOK TIME: 8 TO 10
HOURS ON LOW

INGREDIENTS

- Pork shoulder joint (approx. 1.5 - 2 kg)
    - 2 tbsp. Jerk spice mix
    - 4 cloves garlic, crushed
    - 1 tbsp. light brown sugar
    - 2 red onions
    - Salt and pepper to season

PINEAPPLE SALSA

- 1 x small fresh pineapple 1 red onion
    - 1 red chilli
    - 1 green chilli Juice of ½ lime
    - Fresh mint leaves - optional

Notes

You can also use diced pork, just reduce the cooking time to 6 to 8 hours on low or 4 to 6 hours on high.

METHOD

1. Pierce holes in the pork shoulder joint and insert the crushed garlic inside.

2. Rub the jerk spice mix, sugar, salt and pepper over the pork joint. Optionally marinate it overnight.

3. Add the pork to the slow cooker and place the red onion chunks around it on the base.

4. Cook on low for 8 to 10 hours.

5. At the end of the cooking time, check the pork is cooked through. Remove it from the slow cooker and place it on a chopping board or in a bowl. Use 2 forks to pull the meat apart and return shredded meat to the slow cooker, stirring it round to mix.

6. Serve in brioche buns with pineapple salsa and potato wedges.

MAKING THE PINEAPPLE SALSA

1. Peel, core and finely dice the pineapple.

2. Chop the ends from the chillies, deseed if you prefer a milder taste, finely slice them.

3. Finely chop the onion and fresh mint leaves if using.

4. In a bowl, mix all the ingredients together, pouring the lime juice over the ingredients at the end. It will last in an airtight container for up to 3 days in the fridge.

PULLED CURRIED PORK

SERVINGS: 4

PREP TIME: 20 MINUTES

COOK TIME: 8 TO 10
HOURS ON LOW

INGREDIENTS

- 1.5-2 kg boneless pork joint
- 1 tbsp. curry powder

- FOR THE SAUCE*

- 1 tbsp. oil
- 3 cloves garlic, crushed
- 1 tbsp. fresh root ginger, grated/1 tsp ground ginger
- 1 tbsp. curry powder
- ½ tsp dried chilli flakes
- 2 tbsp. tomato puree
- 1 tbsp. light brown sugar
- ½ tsp salt
- ½ tsp pepper
- 150ml water
- 100ml yoghurt

METHOD

1. Rub the curry powder over the pork.

2. If you are making your own curry sauce, heat the oil in a pan and gently fry the garlic and ginger - just for 1 minute.

3. Add the curry powder, chilli flakes, tomato puree and cook for a further minute.

4. Add the sugar, salt, pepper, water and yoghurt. Continue to simmer on low heat for 3 minutes, continuously stirring it until the liquid has reduced and thickened.

5. Place the pork joint in the slow cooker and pour the curry sauce over the top.

6. Set off on low for 8 - 10 hours.

7. Using 2 forks, pull the pork apart and mix it in with the sauce.

8. Serve in tortilla wraps, with some naan bread, or over rice.

Notes

For a super speedy meal, grab a jar of premade curry sauce and use this instead!

GAMMON

SERVINGS: NA

PREP TIME: 20 MINUTES

COOK TIME: 6 TO 8
HOURS ON LOW

INGREDIENTS

- 1kg - 2kg gammon joint (smoked or unsmoked)
- 1 onion
- Cloves/peppercorns
- 250ml water*

METHOD

1. Place gammon joint in the slow cooker.

2. Add chopped up onion (and any other vegetables), and peppercorns around the gammon.

3. Pour in water (or your chosen liquid)Place lid on the slow cooker and set off for 4 hours on high, or 6-8 hours on low.

4. Remove the gammon from the slow cooker and leave to stand before carving (unless you are adding a glaze) - serve hot or cold.

5. Optional glaze: score the gammon joint and rub some honey over the top. You can also mix in some sugar and/or mustard. Place in a preheated oven (200C/Gas Mark 7) and cook for 10 to 15 minutes.

Notes

*You can swap the water for either; cola, apple juice, pineapple juice or dry cider.

PORK CASSEROLE

SERVINGS: NA

PREP TIME: 20 MINUTES

COOK TIME: 6 TO 8
HOURS ON LOW

INGREDIENTS

- 4 boneless pork chops/500g - 750g diced pork
- 1 onion, sliced
- 2 cloves garlic, crushed
- 1 tsp Dijon mustard
- 400g chopped tomatoes
- 1 tbsp. tomato puree
- 2 carrots, chopped
- 1 leek, chopped
- 2 bay leaves
- 1 tsp dried thyme
- 100ml vegetable/chicken stock
- Salt and pepper to taste

METHOD

1. Add all the ingredients to the slow cooker apart from the pork and mix together.

2. Add the pork and submerge it in the mix.

3. Set off on low for 6-8 hrs, or high for 5-6 hrs.

4. Remove the bay leaves and serve with mashed potato or rice.

Notes

Substitute with any vegetables you have available. If you add in any softer green vegetables such as courgette and broccoli add them 20 to 30 minutes before the end to avoid them going too soft.

CHAPTER 7

LAMB RECIPES

LAMB CURRY

SERVINGS: 4

PREP TIME: 10 MINUTES

COOK TIME: 8 TO 10 HOURS ON LOW

INGREDIENTS

- 600g lamb, diced
- 2 onions, chopped
- 3 garlic cloves, crushed
- 1tbsp fresh ginger, grated (or 1tsp ground ginger)
- 6 tbsp. curry paste*
- 2 tsp ground cumin
- 1 tsp ground cinnamon
- 4 tbsp. tomato puree
- 400g tomatoes (fresh or tinned)
- 1 vegetable stock cube dissolved in 50ml water*
- Handful of baby spinach (optional)

METHOD

1. Mix all the ingredients together in the slow cooker, apart from the spinach, if using.

2. Set off on low for 6-8 hours, or until the lamb is soft and tender. If you are adding spinach, lift the lid and stir in and leave to cook for a further 20 minutes.

3. Serve with rice and naan bread.

Notes

Curry Paste - you can use your favourite curry paste for this, madras is a popular one with lamb, but if it's too hot, use a milder one such as korma. You can also make your own curry paste if you have the time or inclination!

LAMB SHANKS

SERVINGS: 4

PREP TIME: 10 MINUTES

COOK TIME: 8
HOURS ON LOW

INGREDIENTS

- 4 lamb shanks
- 2 large carrots, chopped
- 1 onion, sliced
- 4 cloves garlic, crushed
- 2 bay leaves
- 1 tsp dried mixed herbs
- 400g passata/chopped tomatoes
- 500ml beef stock
- 1 tbsp. Worcestershire sauce
- 2 tbsp. tomato puree

METHOD

1. Add lamb shanks to the slow cooker.

2. Add carrots, onion, garlic, bay leaves and mixed herbs.

3. Pour passata or chopped tomatoes over the top.

4. Stir tomato puree and Worcestershire sauce into beef stock and pour over the lamb shanks.

5. Set off on high for 3 to 4 hours or low for 8 hours.

6. If the sauce is too thin, leave the lid off for 30 minutes, or transfer the sauce to a pan and boil until it thickens.

LAMB TAGINE

SERVINGS: 4

PREP TIME: 10 MINUTES

COOK TIME: 8 TO 10 HOURS ON LOW

INGREDIENTS

- 600g lamb, diced
- 1 onion, sliced
- 3 cloves garlic, crushed
- 1 tbsp. fresh root ginger, grated/1tsp ground ginger
- 1 tsp ground cinnamon
- 1 tbsp. Harissa chilli paste
- 200g dried apricots
- 1 tbsp. runny honey
- 400g tin chickpeas, drained and rinsed
- 400g tin chopped tomatoes
- 250ml lamb or chicken stock seasoning according to taste

METHOD

1. Add everything to the slow cooker and stir together.

2. Cook on low for 8-10 hours, or high for 4, until lamb is tender.

MOROCCAN LAMB WRAPS

SERVINGS: 4

PREP TIME: 10 MINUTES

COOK TIME: 6
HOURS ON LOW

INGREDIENTS

- 500g-750g minced lamb
- 2 red onions, sliced
- 2 tbsp. Ras El Hanout seasoning*
- 1 tbsp. tomato puree 100g Bulgar wheat or couscous
- 500ml hot lamb/vegetable stock

METHOD

1. Make up the hot lamb stock (you can substitute this with vegetable or beef stock if you don't have any lamb).

2. Add the Ras El Hanout seasoning (or alternative spices if using) and tomato puree. Mix together.

3. Add the lamb, chopped onions and bulgur wheat/couscous to the slow cooker.

4. Pour the stock mixture over the top and gently stir. Set off on low for 6 hours.

5. Serve in warmed tortilla wraps with lettuce and hummus.

Notes

*Ras El Hanout - if you can't find any of this spice blend, substitute with 1 tsp ground cinnamon, 2 tsp ground cumin, 1 tsp chilli powder, 1 tsp ground ginger.

LANCASHIRE HOTPOT

SERVINGS: 4

PREP TIME: 20 MINUTES

COOK TIME: 6 TO 8
HOURS ON LOW

INGREDIENTS

- 600g diced lamb
- 50g plain flour
- 1 medium onions, sliced
- 2 cloves garlic, crushed
- 2 carrots, finely sliced
- 2 celery sticks, finely sliced
- 2 tsp dried mixed herbs
- 1 tbsp. Worcestershire sauce
- 400ml beef stock
- 500g potatoes, peeled and thinly sliced
- 50g butter
- Salt and pepper to season

METHOD

1. Coat the lamb with the flour.

2. Add all the ingredients to the slow cooker, apart from the potatoes and butter.

3. Pour the beef stock over the top of the lamb and vegetables.

4. Cover with the potato slices and dot with the butter.

5. Cook on low for 6 to 8 hours, or high for 3 to 4 hours.

6. Serving Suggestion: tastes great by itself, or with some cabbage.

LAMB KEEMA

SERVINGS: 4

PREP TIME: 10 MINUTES

COOK TIME: 8 TO 10
HOURS ON LOW

INGREDIENTS

- 500g-750g lamb mince
- 2 onions, chopped
- 3 garlic cloves, crushed
- 2 tsp ground coriander
- 2 tsp ground turmeric
- 1 tbsp. garam masala
- 1 tbsp. fresh root ginger, grated/1tsp of ground ginger
- 1 tsp chilli powder
- 400g chopped tomatoes
- 2 large potatoes, chopped
- 200g frozen peas*

METHOD

1. Mix spices and chopped tomatoes together.

2. Apart from the frozen peas, add everything to the slow cooker pot and stir well to mix together.

3. Set off on low for 8 to 10 hours. 30 minutes before the end stir in the frozen peas (and/or spinach leaves if you are using).

Notes

Swap minced lamb for minced beef if you wish.
Substitute the peas for some baby spinach leaves.

Use new potatoes, sweet potatoes or any kind of potato you prefer!

JAMAICAN LAMB CURRY

SERVINGS: 4

PREP TIME: 10 MINUTES

COOK TIME: 8 - 10 HOURS ON LOW

INGREDIENTS

- 600g lamb, diced 1 onion, sliced
- 3 cloves garlic, crushed
- 1 or 2 x scotch bonnet chillies*, finely sliced
- 1 red bell pepper, sliced
- 1 tbsp. fresh root ginger, grated/1 tsp ground ginger
- 1 tbsp. curry powder
- 1 tsp turmeric
- 1 tsp ground allspice
- 1 tsp ground cloves
- 1 tsp dried thyme
- ½ tsp ground cinnamon (or 1 cinnamon stick)
- 400g chopped tomatoes
- 1 tbsp. brown sugar
- 1 chicken stock cube/pot in 100ml boiling water seasoning according to taste

METHOD

1. Add all the ingredients to the slow cooker and mix them together.

2. Set off on high for 4 - 6 hours, or low for 8-10 hours.

3. Serve with rice or potatoes.

Notes

Although Scotch Bonnets aren't the hottest chilli you can get, they are very hot. If you prefer milder heat, just add 1, or opt for a bird's eye or red pepper. Either way, be careful when handling them, use gloves if you can and keep them well away from your eyes!

LAMB IN MINT SAUCE

SERVINGS: 4 - 6

PREP TIME: 10 MINUTES

COOK TIME: 6
HOURS ON LOW

INGREDIENTS

- 1.5kg to 2kg lamb shoulder
- 4 tbsp. mint sauce
- Salt and pepper to season
- 2 sprigs fresh rosemary
- 400ml lamb/vegetable stock

METHOD

1. Add the lamb joint to the slow cooker and season with salt and pepper according to taste. Brush the mint sauce over the lamb.

2. Pour stock around the lamb joint and lay rosemary sprigs on top.

3. Place lid on and set off on low for 6 hours. Remove lamb from slow cooker and optionally roast in the oven for 10 - 15 minutes while you make the gravy.

4. The gravy will likely need thickening up. Skim off the layer of fat from the surface and transfer to a saucepan and add a corn flour slurry (1 tbsp. corn flour mixed with 2 tbsp. water) - simmer until reduced and thickened.

Notes

Optionally add in some vegetables so that you have a complete meal to serve! Chopped carrots, and new potatoes work well. If you are adding green vegetables, add these in the last 30 minutes.

It also tastes amazing in a giant Yorkshire pudding!

LAMB & GUINNESS CASSEROLE

SERVINGS: 4

PREP TIME: 20 MINUTES

COOK TIME: 7 TO 8
HOURS ON LOW

INGREDIENTS

- 600g lamb, cubed
- 1 tbsp. tomato puree
- 1 medium onion, chopped
- 3 cloves of garlic, crushed
- 1 tsp dried mixed herbs
- 1 tbsp. mustard
- 1 tbsp. Worcestershire sauce
- 4 medium carrots, chopped
- 1 large potato, peeled and cubed
- 200g frozen peas
- 200ml beef stock
- 400ml Guinness or any other stout or ale

METHOD

1. Add all the ingredients to the slow cooker (apart from the peas) and stir to combine.

2. Cook on low for 7 to 8 hours, or high for 4 to 5 hours. About 30 minutes before the end add in the peas.

3. Serving suggestion: serve with crusty bread.

CURRIED LAMB & LENTILS

SERVINGS: 4

PREP TIME: 20 MINUTES

COOK TIME: 6 TO 8
HOURS ON LOW

INGREDIENTS

- 600g lamb, diced or minced
- 1 medium onion, chopped
- 2 cloves garlic, crushed
- 1 scotch bonnet (or other red chilli), sliced
- 1 tbsp. mild curry powder
- 1 tbsp. fresh root ginger, grated/1 tsp ground ginger
- 2 tbsp. tomato puree
- 400g tin chopped tomatoes
- 200g red lentils, rinsed
- 200ml lamb/vegetable/chicken stock seasoning

METHOD

1. Add everything to the slow cooker pot and cook on low for 6 to 8 hours or 3 to 4 hours on high, until the lamb is soft and tender.

2. Serve with green salad, rice, couscous, new potatoes, or just as it is.

Notes

Chillies: scotch bonnets are very hot so use a milder chilli if you prefer, or leave it out completely if you wish. Remember to be very careful when handling chillies - wear gloves if you can!

CHAPTER 8

FISH RECIPES

Coconut Fish Curry

Salmon & Dill

Thai Curried Cod

COCONUT FISH CURRY

SERVINGS: 4

PREP TIME: 20 MINUTES

COOK TIME: 2 TO 3
HOURS ON LOW

INGREDIENTS

- 400-600g white fish*
- 1 onion, chopped
- 2 cloves garlic, crushed
- 1 tbsp. fresh root ginger, grated/1 tsp ground ginger
- 1-2 red chillies, sliced
- 1 tsp garam masala
- 1 tsp turmeric
- 400ml coconut milk
- 150ml vegetable stock
- 2 lemongrass stalks**, bashed
- 200g mange tout/broccoli/frozen peas

METHOD

1. Add the coconut milk, vegetable stock, ginger, garam masala and turmeric to the slow cooker and mix together.

2. Add the onion, garlic, chillies and lemongrass.

3. 20 - 30 minutes before the end, add in your choice of vegetable (mange tout/broccoli/frozen peas)

4. Gently place the fish in the mixture, place lid on and set off on low for 2 - 3 hours. Remove lemongrass.

Notes

*You can use any firm white fish such as cod, haddock, pollock, hake etc.

**If you don't have any lemongrass substitute with the zest of 1 lemon.

SALMON & DILL

SERVINGS: 4

PREP TIME: 5 MINUTES

COOK TIME: 2
HOURS ON LOW

INGREDIENTS

- 4 salmon fillets
- 1 unwaxed lemon, sliced 1 tsp dried herbs
- 250ml water (or stock, cider, wine)

METHOD

1. Place some baking paper at the bottom of the slow cooker to act as a sling for the salmon - making it easier to lift the salmon out once cooked.

2. Lay the salmon fillets on top, side by side.

3. Add the sliced lemons across each salmon and seasoning with the dried herbs

4. Add your choice of liquid (pour down the sides of the salmons to try and not wash the lemon slices and seasoning off the top).

5. Cook on low for 2 hours. At the end of the cooking time, lift the salmon out using the baking paper sling to prevent it from falling apart.

THAI CURRIED COD

SERVINGS: 4

PREP TIME: 10 MINUTES

COOK TIME: 2
HOURS ON LOW

INGREDIENTS

- 400ml coconut milk
- 4 tbsp. Thai Red Curry Paste
- 1 tbsp. grated fresh ginger/1 tsp ground ginger
- 2 cloves garlic, crushed Spring onions/fresh basil (optional garnish)

METHOD

1. Add coconut milk, curry paste, ginger and garlic to the slow cooker and stir together until well combined.

2. Submerge cod in the sauce. Optionally add the peppers in now or, for a firmer texture, add them in 30 minutes before the end of the cooking time.

3. Set off on low for 2 hours.

4. Serve with rice.

CHAPTER 9

NON MEAT RECIPES

BUTTERNUT SQUASH & LENTIL CURRY

SERVINGS: 4

PREP TIME: 15 MINUTES

COOK TIME: 6
HOURS ON LOW

INGREDIENTS

- 300g dried red lentils, rinsed
- 1 large butternut squash, peeled, cubed
- 1 onion, sliced
- 3 cloves garlic, crushed
- 1 tbsp. fresh root ginger, grated
- 1 tbsp. curry powder
- 2 tsp garam masala
- 2 tsp ground cumin
- 400g chopped tomatoes
- 400ml coconut milk
- Salt and pepper to season
- Fresh coriander leaves to garnish

METHOD

1. Add everything to the slow cooker and set it off on low for 6 hours, or high for 3 hours.

2. Garnish with fresh coriander leaves and serve with rice, or as it is.

Notes

Optionally stir in some spinach leaves 20 to 30 minutes before the end.

SMOKY BUTTERBEAN HOT POT

SERVINGS: 4

PREP TIME: 15 MINUTES

COOK TIME: 6 - 8
HOURS ON LOW

INGREDIENTS

- 1 red onion, chopped
- 2 garlic cloves, chopped
- 1 tbsp. smoked paprika
- 2 celery sticks, chopped
- 2 carrots, chopped
- 3 medium potatoes, cut into chunks
- 1 red pepper, chopped
- 1 x 400g tin butter beans, drained, rinsed
- 1 x 400g tin tomatoes, or fresh tomatoes
- 2 tbsp. tomato puree
- 250ml vegetable stock
- 100g kale or baby leaf spinach
- Seasoning

METHOD

1. Add all the ingredients to the slow cooker (apart from the spinach/kale) and mix together.

2. Cook on low for 6 to 8 hours, or high for 4 hours. 20 to 30 minutes before the end of the cook time add the spinach/kale).

3. Serving Suggestion: serve with crusty bread.

MIXED BEAN CHILLI

SERVINGS: 4

PREP TIME: 10 MINUTES

COOK TIME: 6 TO 8
HOURS ON LOW

INGREDIENTS

- 2 red onions, sliced
- 3 cloves garlic, crushed 3 tsp chipotle paste
- 1 tsp smoked paprika
- ½ tsp ground cinnamon
- 1 tsp ground cumin
- 1 tsp ground coriander
- 1 sweet pepper, sliced
- 400g chopped tomatoes
- 2 x 400g of mixed beans, rinsed and drained*
- Salt and pepper to taste

METHOD

1. Add all the ingredients to the slow cooker and stir together.

2. Place the lid on and set off on low for 6 to 8 hours, or high for 3 - 4 hours.

3. At the end of the cooking time, if required, add some more seasoning according to taste. If you want some more spice, stir in some dried chilli flakes.

4. Serve with rice and sour cream, or guacamole. It also tastes great on top of a jacket potato or on a tortilla wrap.

Notes

* You can either use tins of mixed beans or mix and match your favourites/what you have available. Options include; chickpeas, kidney beans, black-eyed beans, haricot etc.

MACARONI CHEESE

SERVINGS: 4

PREP TIME: 10 MINUTES

COOK TIME: 1.5-2
HOURS ON LOW

INGREDIENTS

- 500g macaroni pasta
- 1L whole milk
- 250ml double cream
- 3 tbsp. butter
- 150g cheddar cheese, grated
- 75g parmesan cheese, grated
- 2 cloves garlic, crushed
- 1 tsp dried mixed herbs
- 1 tsp black pepper
- ½ tsp English mustard powder

METHOD

1. Add everything to the slow cooker and mix it all together.

2. Place the lid on and set off on low for 2 hours.

3. At the 1.5 hour mark lift the lid and give everything a good stir - try and do this as quickly as possible so as not to lose too much heat from the slow cooker. If the sauce has thickened up enough by this point, you can turn it off and serve. If it needs some more time, put the lid back on and cook for a further 30 minutes.

Notes

If the sauce becomes too dry, stir in some milk to loosen it up. When it is cooked, optionally sprinkle some breadcrumbs and grated cheddar cheese on top and grill for 5 to 10 minutes.

CHICKPEA CURRY

SERVINGS: 4

PREP TIME: 10 MINUTES

COOK TIME: 6 TO 8
HOURS ON LOW

INGREDIENTS

- 1 onion, chopped
- 3 cloves garlic, crushed
- 2 tbsp. curry powder
- 2 x 400g chickpeas, rinsed and drained
- 2 x 400g chopped tomatoes/ passata
- 2 sweet peppers, deseeded and sliced
- 2 large potatoes*, peeled and diced
- 1/2 tsp salt
- 1/2 tsp black pepper

METHOD

1. Add all the ingredients to the slow cooker and stir together.

2. Set off on low for 6 to 8 hours.

3. Serve with rice and a green salad.

Notes

Substitute the potatoes with butternut squash or sweet potato if preferred.

BLACK BEAN STEW

SERVINGS: 4 - 6

PREP TIME: 10 MINUTES

COOK TIME: 6
HOURS ON LOW

INGREDIENTS

- 400g tin black beans, drained and rinsed
- 1 onion, sliced
- 3 cloves garlic, crushed
- 1 sweet pepper, sliced
- 1 tbsp. chilli powder
- 2 tsp ground cumin
- 2 tsp smoked paprika
- ½ tsp salt
- 400g passata
- 120g quinoa (uncooked)
- 1 litre vegetable stock
- Fresh coriander, optional garnish

METHOD

1. Add everything to the slow cooker and stir together.

2. Set off on low for 6 hours, or high for 4 hours.

LENTIL BOLOGNESE

 SERVINGS: 4

 PREP TIME: 10 MINUTES

 COOK TIME: 8 HOURS ON LOW

INGREDIENTS

- 200g green lentils*
- 2 x 400g passata
- 1 onion, sliced
- 2 cloves garlic, crushed
- 2 celery stalks, finely sliced
- 250ml vegetable stock
- ½ tsp dried chilli flakes
- ½ tsp black pepper
- ½ tsp salt
- Cooked pasta to serve

METHOD

1. Add everything to the slow cooker and stir together.

2. Set off on low for 8 hours or high for 4 hours.

3. At the end of the cooking time stir in cooked pasta and optionally add some grated cheese.

Notes
*Substitute with red lentils if preferred.

JACKET POTATOES

SERVINGS: 4

PREP TIME: 5 MINUTES

COOK TIME: 8 HOURS ON LOW

INGREDIENTS

- ◆ 4 baking potatoes
- ◆ Oil
- ◆ Salt

METHOD

1. Wash your baking potato thoroughly, scrubbing the skin.

2. Dry using some kitchen towel or a tea towel. Pierce all over with a fork.

3. Run some oil over each potato and then a little salt.

4. Wrap in foil and place in the slow cooker

5. Put the lid on and set off on high for 4-5 hours, or low for 7-8 hours. The potato should be soft and fluffy in the middle when it is ready.

6. For a crispy skin put them in the oven for 5 minutes before serving. Cut open and add your favourite toppings!

Notes
Try switching the baking potatoes for sweet potatoes!

SMOKED PAPRIKA POTATOES

SERVINGS: 4

PREP TIME: 10 MINUTES

COOK TIME: 4
HOURS ON HIGH

INGREDIENTS

- 400g chopped tomatoes
- 1 tbsp. Worcestershire sauce
- 3 cloves garlic, crushed
- 1 red onion, diced
- 1 tsp dried chilli flakes
- 1 tbsp. smoked paprika
- 1 red pepper, sliced
- 400ml vegetable stock
- 800g potatoes, diced

METHOD

1. Add all the ingredients to the slow cooker apart from the potatoes. Mix together until well combined.

2. Add the diced potatoes to the mixture and submerge them.

3. Put the lid on and cook for 4 hours on high, or until the potatoes are soft and cooked through.

Notes

Maris pipers or baking potatoes are the best variety to use.

SWEET POTATO CURRY

SERVINGS: 4

PREP TIME: 20 MINUTES

COOK TIME: 6 TO 8
HOURS ON LOW

INGREDIENTS

- 1 onion, chopped
- 2 cloves garlic, crushed
- 800g sweet potato, peeled and chopped
- 300g dried red lentils, rinsed
- 1 tbsp. fresh root ginger, grated/1 tsp ground ginger
- 4 tbsp. curry paste*
- 1 tsp ground turmeric
- 1 tsp ground cumin
- 4 tbsp. tomato puree
- 1 x 400g tin coconut milk
- 800ml vegetable stock
- Handful baby spinach leaves
- Salt and pepper to season

METHOD

1. Add everything to the slow cooker apart from the spinach.

2. Set off on low for 6 to 8 hours, or high for 3 to 4 hours. 20 to 30 minutes before the end of the cooking time stir in the spinach leaves.

3. Serve with rice, quinoa, or naan bread.

Notes

Curry paste - add less or more depending on how much spice you like. Thai red curry paste works well with this curry, as does any Indian curry paste.

CHILLI STUFFED PEPPERS

SERVINGS: 4

PREP TIME: 10 MINUTES

COOK TIME: 4 TO 5
HOURS ON LOW

INGREDIENTS

- 4-6 sweet bell peppers (any colours)
- 1 onion, finely sliced
- 2 cloves garlic, crushed
- 1 tsp chilli powder
- 1 tsp ground cumin
- 1 tsp ground coriander
- 400g tin red kidney beans or black beans, drained
- 400g chopped tomatoes
- 200g quinoa (uncooked), or cooked brown rice

METHOD

1. Slice the tops off the peppers and remove the seeds and stem from the inside, taking care not to split the pepper.

2. In a bowl, mix together the onion, garlic, spices, beans, chopped tomatoes and rice/quinoa.

3. Scoop the mixture into the peppers.

4. Put a little water in the base of the slow cooker and place the peppers in the slow cooker in an upright position.

5. Put the lid on top and set off on low for 4 to 5 hours, or high for 3 hours.

6. Optionally serve with chopped coriander on top, sour cream, or melt some cheese on top.

Notes

* You can either use tins of mixed beans or mix and match your favourites/what you have available. Options include; chickpeas, kidney beans, black- eyed beans, haricot etc.

TOMATO PINTO BEANS

SERVINGS: 4-6

PREP TIME: 12 HOURS/
OVERNIGHT

COOK TIME: 8 TO 10
HOURS ON LOW

INGREDIENTS

- 500g pinto beans
- 1 red onion, finely diced
- 1 clove garlic, crushed
- 1 tbsp. smoked paprika
- 1 tbsp. white wine or apple cider vinegar
- 50g light brown sugar
- 400ml tomato passata
- 4 tbsp. tomato puree
- 50g butter
- ½ tsp salt

METHOD

1. Cover the pinto beans in water and soak them overnight.

2. In the morning, rapid boil the beans for 10 minutes, or according to packet instructions. If the beans have soaked up all the water overnight add some more.

3. Add everything to the slow cooker, including the water, and stir together.

4. Cook on low for 8 to 10 hours.

Notes

Pinto beans can be substituted for cannellini beans or any other dried bean.

CHAPTER 10

PUDDINGS, BAKES & DRINKS RECIPES

APPLE CRUMBLE

SERVINGS: 4 - 6

PREP TIME: 15 MINUTES

COOK TIME: 3
HOURS ON HIGH

INGREDIENTS

CRUMBLE

- 180g plain flour
- 180g rolled oats
- 100g granulated sugar (demerara is good, or caster)
- 150g butter
- 1 tsp ground cinnamon

FILLING

- 4 cooking apples, peeled and cored
- 1 tsp ground cinnamon
- 1 tsp mixed spice

METHOD

1. In a bowl using your hands, mix together the flour, oats, sugar, butter and cinnamon until the ingredients resemble bread crumbs.

2. Peel, core and chop the apples into chunks. Lay across the bottom of the slow cooker bowl. Sprinkle the ground ginger and mixed spices on top.

4. Sprinkle the crumble mixture on top of the apples.

5. Put the lid on and cook on high for 3 hours. Leave the lid off for the last 30 minutes of cooking time to crisp up the crumble.

6. Serving Suggestion: Tastes delicious with custard or vanilla ice cream.

HOT CHOCOLATE

SERVINGS: 8

PREP TIME: 5 MINUTES

COOK TIME: 2
HOURS ON LOW

INGREDIENTS

- 1 litre milk (whole)
- 250ml double cream
- 100g dark chocolate
- 100g milk chocolate
- 1 tbsp. vanilla extract
- Marshmallows, grated chocolate and whipped cream to serve

METHOD

1. Break up the chocolate and add everything to the slow cooker.

2. Add the lid and cook on low for 2 to 2.5 hours.

3. After 1 hour lift the lid and stir and then again 30 minutes later.

4. Serve in mugs with marshmallows, chocolate shavings and whipped cream.

APPLE AND RAISIN BREAD PUDDING

SERVINGS: 6

PREP TIME:

COOK TIME: 2 TO 3
HOURS ON LOW

INGREDIENTS

- 400g apples (Bramley work well), peeled, cored, cubed
- 2 tbsp. lemon juice
- 200g raisins
- 10 slices of bread, cut into ½ inch cubes
- 2 tsp ground cinnamon
- 2 tsp vanilla essence
- 150g brown sugar
- 150g melted butter

METHOD

1. Place the apple chunks, lemon juice and raisins in the slow cooker pot. Sprinkle 1 tsp of cinnamon over the top.

2. Lay the bread cubes over the top.

3. In a separate bowl, mix together the melted butter, sugar, vanilla essence and remaining cinnamon.

4. Pour the melted butter mixture over the top, coating all of the bread.

5. Put the lid on the slow cooker pot and cook on low for 2 to 3 hours.

CHOCOLATE LAVA CAKE

SERVINGS: 6

PREP TIME: 20 MINUTES

COOK TIME: LOW FOR
3 TO 4 HOURS

INGREDIENTS

- 250g self-raising flour
- 200g granulated sugar
- 8 tbsp. cocoa powder
- Pinch salt
- 200ml milk
- 150g butter, melted
- 2 tsp vanilla extract
- 50g light brown sugar
- 300ml hot water

METHOD

1. Lightly grease the slow cooker with butter or a non-stick spray.

2. In a bowl, whisk together the flour, granulated sugar, 6tbsp cocoa powder and salt.

3. Make a well in the middle of the dry ingredients and add the milk, butter and vanilla extract. Whisk it until smooth.

4. Transfer the batter directly to the slow cooker. Sprinkle the brown sugar directly on top of the batter in the slow cooker, followed by the 2 remaining tablespoons of cocoa powder.

5. Finally, pour the hot water over the top of everything, don't stir it in.

6. Put the lid on the slow cooker and set it off on low for 3 to 4 hours.

BANANA BREAD

SERVINGS: 8

PREP TIME: 20 MINUTES

COOK TIME: 2 TO 3
HOURS ON HIGH

INGREDIENTS

- 200g strong white flour, (you can also use plain flour)
- 2 tsp baking powder
- 2 tsp cinnamon
- 3 ripe bananas, mashed
- 2 eggs, beaten
- 100ml vegetable oil
- 150g soft brown sugar
- 1 tsp vanilla extract

METHOD

1. Lightly grease a loaf tin (make sure it can fit in your slow cooker)

2. In a large bowl, sift the flour, cinnamon and baking powder and mix together.

3. Mix the beaten eggs with the mashed bananas. Add in the oil, sugar and vanilla extract.

4. Make a well in the bowl containing the flour. Slowly pour in the egg mixture, stirring gently until all the ingredients are blended together. Do not mix too much, just until it is smooth.

5. Add the mixture to your greased loaf tin. Place the tin into your slow cooker. Put a tea towel under the lid to stop any condensation dripping back down onto the bread and making it soggy.

6. Cook on high for 2 to 3 hours. When it is ready you should be able to insert a skewer into the centre and it comes out clean. Allow to cool for a bit before removing from the tin and then transfer to a wire rack to cool some more.

RICE PUDDING

SERVINGS: 4

PREP TIME: 5 MINUTES

COOK TIME: 3 TO 4
HOURS ON HIGH

INGREDIENTS

- 125g pudding rice
- 2 pints milk (full fat)
- 30g caster sugar
- 30g butter
- ½ tsp ground cinnamon
- 1 tsp vanilla extract

METHOD

1. Place the pudding rice, sugar, butter and cinnamon in the slow cooker bowl. Pour in the milk and mix well.

2. Cook on high for 3 to 4 hours or until the rice is soft and soaked in all the milk.

Notes

To make coconut rice pudding: add 50g desiccated coconut at the start.
To make chocolate rice pudding: add 3 tbsp. cocoa powder and stir in at the start.
To make it even creamier: add 1 tin of condensed milk (397g) at the start.
Top with fresh berries, jam, chocolate chips or a sprinkling of desiccated coconut.

PORRIDGE

SERVINGS: 4

PREP TIME: 5 MINUTES

COOK TIME: 3 TO 8
HOURS ON LOW

INGREDIENTS

- 200g jumbo rolled oats
- 800ml milk or water (or a combination of both)
- Salt (optional)
- Cinnamon (optional)

METHOD

1. Mix oats and liquid together, either directly in the slow cooker (grease the bowl first with a little butter or oil), or in a large casserole dish and place that in the slow cooker. If you are using a bowl within the slow cooker bowl, you can add some water around it too.

2. If you are adding salt or cinnamon stir this in too.

3. Cook on low for between 3 and 8 hours. Use a timer or keep warm function if needed. Stir the porridge before serving with your favourite toppings on top.

Notes

The longer you leave the porridge cooking the softer and creamier it will be. The first time you make it, do it in the day time when you are there to check it doesn't overcook when left for too long!

CHOCOLATE FUDGE

PREP TIME: 20 MINUTES

COOK TIME: 1 HOUR 30
ON LOW

CHILL TIME: 3 HOURS

INGREDIENTS

- 2 tbsp. vanilla essence
- 2 tbsp. butter
- 397g condensed milk, (1 tin)
- 350g milk chocolate

METHOD

1. Break up all the chocolate into squares and add to the slow cooker.

2. Add the other ingredients.

3. Switch your slow cooker on low. Leave the lid off. Cook for around 90 minutes, stirring every 15 minutes with a wooden spoon.

4. Pour the mixture into a lined baking tin (I used 20cm) and allow to cool.

5. Transfer to the fridge to set (at least 3 hours).6. Remove from the fridge and chop up into chunks.

Notes

Experiment with different flavours - use white chocolate instead of milk, or add in some peanut butter for a delicious twist on the taste!

CHOCOLATE BROWNIES

SERVINGS: 16

PREP TIME: 20 MINUTES

COOK TIME: 3
HOURS ON LOW

INGREDIENTS

- 300g dark cooking chocolate
- 180g butter
- 120g plain flour
- 40g cocoa powder
- 250g sugar
- 3 eggs

METHOD

1. Cut the butter into cubes and break up the chocolate bar. Place in a bowl, and place that bowl over a saucepan of boiling water (this melts the chocolate and butter gently and avoids burning it). The bowl should rest on the saucepan and not be in the water. Melt the butter and chocolate together, stirring with a spoon.

2. Transfer to a bowl, and whisk in the eggs, one at a time. Sift in the flour and cocoa powder, and add the sugar. Mix to form a smooth mixture.

3. Line the slow cooker bowl with baking paper, and transfer the mix to the bowl. Flatten out with a knife or spoon, place a tea towel under the lid, and cook on low for 3 hours.

APPLE & CINNAMON CAKE

SERVINGS: 6

PREP TIME: 20 MINUTES

COOK TIME: 3
HOURS ON HIGH

INGREDIENTS

- 170g self-raising flour
- 170g butter, softened
- 170g light brown sugar
- 3 eggs, beaten
- 2 tsp cinnamon
- 1 tbsp. milk
- 2 Bramley apples

METHOD

1. In a bowl mix together the flour, butter, sugar, cinnamon, eggs and milk.

2. Peel and dice the apples. Mix the apples into the cake batter.

3. Lightly grease the cake tin or pudding bowl and transfer the cake mixture into it.

4. Place the cake tin in the slow cooker and pour boiling water into the slow cooker pot, so that it comes about halfway up the side.

5. Put a tea towel under the lid of the slow cooker, or wrap foil over the top of the tin. This prevents condensation from dripping down during the cooking time.

6. Set off on high for 3 hours - check that a skewer comes out clean. Leave to cool for 10 minutes before removing. Serve with custard or ice cream

Notes
Do I need to use a tin?

No, you don't have to cook it in the baking tin - you can cook it directly in the slow cooker, just make sure you grease it well. You might need to adjust the quantities slightly depending on the size of your slow cooker.

TREACLE SPONGE PUDDING

SERVINGS: 10

PREP TIME: 20 MINUTES

COOK TIME: 4
HOURS ON HIGH

INGREDIENTS

- 4 tbsp. golden syrup (+ extra for drizzling)
- 175g golden caster sugar 175g self-raising flour
- 1 teaspoon baking powder 175g butter, softened
- 3 eggs, beaten
- 2 tbsp. milk
- 1 tsp vanilla essence

Notes

You will also need:

1 x 1 L pudding bowl, foil.

METHOD

1. Lightly grease the pudding bowl.

2. Add the golden syrup to the bottom of the pudding bowl.

3. In a mixing bowl, combine and mix the sugar, flour, baking powder, butter, eggs, milk and vanilla essence. Stir until well mixed.

4. Pour sponge mixture on top of the syrup in the pudding bowl.

5. Put foil over the top of the pudding bowl.

6. Place the pudding bowl in the slow cooker. Add enough water so that it comes about halfway up the side of the pudding bowl.

7. Place the lid on the slow cooker and cook on high for 4 hours.

8. At the end of the cooking time check that the sponge is cooked all the way through by inserting a skewer, if it comes out clean it is ready.

9. Carefully remove the pudding bowl from the slow cooker and on a board or serving plate turn it upside down to remove it from the bowl. Drizzle with more golden syrup if required.

COFFEE CAKE

SERVINGS: 12

PREP TIME: 30 MINUTES

COOK TIME: 2 TO 3
HOURS ON HIGH

INGREDIENTS

CAKE
- 175g butter
- 175g light brown soft sugar
- 175g self-raising flour
- 3 eggs
- 1 tsp baking powder
- 3 tbsp. strong instant coffee, dissolved in 3 tbsp. boiling water*

COFFEE ICING
- 200g icing sugar
- 115g butter, softened
- 1 tsp vanilla extract
- 1 tbsp. milk
- 1 tbsp. strong instant coffee, dissolved in 1 tbsp. boiling water

Notes

*A trivet is a small metal stand. If you don't have one, use scrunched up balls of foil to elevate your tin out of the water.

Use a baking tin that fits in your slow cooker - you can also make it directly in your slow cooker base but you will need to grease it first or use baking paper.

METHOD

1. Cream the butter and sugar together in a mixing bowl.

2. Add the coffee, and mix in the eggs, a little at a time, whisking well in between each addition.

3. Sift in the flour and baking powder, and fold in to form a smooth mixture.

4. Line the base of a loose- bottomed/spring form tin that will fit inside the slow cooker.

5. Transfer the cake mixture to the tin and flatten it down.

6. Pour about half a centimetre of boiling water into the slow cooker, and place the cake tin on a trivet*.

7. Put a tea towel under the lid, and cook on high for 2-3 hours. Do a skewer test in the centre to see if it is done, and if needed, place it back in the slow cooker for another 30 minutes.

8. Prepare the icing by mixing all the icing ingredients together in a bowl until smooth. Ice when the cake is cool, and refrigerate afterwards. Optionally decorate with walnuts.

BREAD

SERVINGS: 10

PREP TIME: 20 MINUTES

COOK TIME: 2
HOURS ON HIGH

INGREDIENTS

- 400g strong white bread flour
- 7g dried active yeast
- 2 tsp salt
- 1 tbsp. sugar
- 250ml warm water
- 2 tbsp. olive oil

METHOD

1. Switch the slow cooker to high.

2. Mix the flour, yeast, salt and sugar in a bowl. Make a well in the middle and slowly add the water and oil, stirring it in as you do.

3. Get your hands in to combine the dough into a ball - to stop the dough sticking to your hands, rub a little oil on them.

4. Sprinkle flour on a worktop counter and knead the dough for about 5 to 10 minutes.

5. Line the slow cooker with some greaseproof paper and place the dough on top.

6. Put the slow cooker lid on top and cook for 2 hours, check on it at the 90 minute mark to see if it is ready (some slow cookers cook faster than others).

7. If you prefer a firmer crust, put it under a grill for 5 minutes.

8. Leave the bread to rest for 10 minutes before slicing.

CHEESECAKE

SERVINGS: 10

PREP TIME: 20 MINUTES

COOK TIME: 5 HOURS ON LOW +
3 HOURS CHILL TIME

INGREDIENTS

BASE

- 150g digestive biscuits
- 100g melted butter

FILLING

- 400g cream cheese
- 200ml double cream
- 100g caster sugar
- 3 eggs
- 2 tsp vanilla extract

METHOD

1. Bash the digestive biscuits up - the easiest way is to put them in a food bag and grab a rolling pin to really crush them down! Alternatively, if you have a food processor you can pulse the biscuits in there.
2. Stir in the melted butter.
3. Lay some baking paper in the base of the slow cooker. Either spray with some non-stick spray, or grease with a little butter.
4. Transfer the biscuit mix into the slow cooker and press down.
5. In a bowl, whisk together the cream cheese, double cream, sugar, eggs and vanilla extract. If you have a food processor you can also use it to get the mixture really smooth.
6. Pour the mixture over the biscuit base. Add a tea towel under the lid of the slow cooker to prevent condensation from falling down on the cheesecake.
7. Set off on low for 5 to 7 hours. The cheesecake is ready when a metal skewer comes out clean.
8. Switch the slow cooker off and leave it to cool down and firm up.
9. When it is cool transfer it to the fridge to chill for at least 3 hours. If you have space in your fridge you can place your whole slow cooker insert in there, or, carefully remove the cheesecake by lifting it out with the baking paper and place it directly in the fridge.
10. After chilling, carefully peel back the baking paper and slice the cheesecake up ready to serve. Optionally drizzle with your favourite sauce (chocolate, strawberry, caramel!) or garnish with some sliced fresh fruits.

Final Words & Acknowledgements

I hope you enjoyed the recipes in this book - I would love to know what you think about any that you made - or, if you have any questions, suggestions or errors to report, please feel free to contact me directly at liana@lianaskitchen.co.uk.

Thanks

I would also like to thank you all for your support for everything that we do at Liana's Kitchen, as well as your continued enthusiasm in the kitchen!

Printed in Great Britain
by Amazon